BEGIN AGAIN

This book is dedicated to

all husbands

Begin Again

A BOOK FOR WOMEN ALONE

Margaret Torrie

WITH A FOREWORD BY
Marjorie Proops

LONDON
J. M. DENT & SONS LTD

Photoset and printed
in Great Britain by
REDWOOD BURN LIMITED
Trowbridge & Esher
for
J. M. DENT & SONS LTD
Aldine House · Albemarle Street London

This book if bound as a Paperback is subject to
the condition that it may not be issued on loan
or otherwise except in its original binding.

First published 1970
Revised edition 1975
First paperback edition 1975
Reprinted 1975

Hardback ISBN: 0 460 04133 9
Paperback ISBN: 0 460 02129 x

CONTENTS

FOREWORD

by Marjorie Proops

My oldest and most beloved friend is a widow. She married latish
in life, in her mid forties, long after—she said—having given up
hope of meeting a man to love who could enrich her lonely life.

After twenty years of marriage he died, and before I telephoned
her I rehearsed the words I wanted to say to offer comfort.

'Don't grieve for me,' she said, before I could spell out those
rehearsed phrases. 'I am so grateful for what we had, for the memories I've got that no one can take away, for having had him to
love, for his love and care for me.'

And in the end, it was she who comforted me.

Brave? Yes, of course. But not only was she brave, she was so
realistic and wise, and today, after several years of widowhood,
her outlook is as it was when her beloved husband died.

She talks of him cheerfully as if he might still walk through the
door saying 'What's for dinner, love?' To her, he still lives. There
has never been a trace of self-pity or a bitter railing against cruel
fate, and she is to me a prime example of a woman who has come
to terms not only with widowhood, but with life, for she sometimes compares her present lone state with her pre-marriage
lonely state, and reminds me how lucky she is. She is not well-off.
She is seriously arthritic, and she thanks God for what she had
and what she's got, which is mainly old snapshots. And memories.

It would be wonderful if every woman alone shared this philo-
sophical attitude, but not all are as strong or as courageous. Many
cannot look back on happiness and treasure memories, for not
every wife can count the blessings of a happy marriage.

Countless widows find it impossible to imagine a future alone.
They are unable to build the bridges or to create the new bridges
which Mrs Torrie, in her splendid book, regards as an essential
link with a new and fulfilling life.

Often newly widowed women withdraw from society, from
family and friends, unable to face what seems like a harsh and indifferent world. And all too often the world *is* harsh and indifferent to the misery of someone once closely dependent on
another human being who has now to cope without support:

moral, emotional and financial. We are all too busy and preoccupied with our own problems, we fail to wonder what kind of despair is hidden by the closed curtains of the widow's home.

Sometimes the despair is brought about by the new and utterly painful isolation. Sometimes it is shortage of cash, or worries about the children, or anxiety over legal difficulties which keep her awake at night. One thing is certain: the lone woman in our world needs kindness and understanding. She needs practical help as well as sympathy to enable her to begin again.

Never was a book more aptly titled than this one, containing as it does such sensible and practical advice along with the deeply caring counselling of the committed author.

The woman in a million, like my friend, may be beautifully adjusted. Sadly, millions are not. Luckily for these, *Begin Again* is their lifeline for survival.

AUTHOR'S INTRODUCTION

The most surprising aspect of my work among widows in the past fourteen years has been the discovery both of the size of the problem and of its general neglect. While all around us we have accepted the mushroom growth of social service and self-help organizations dealing with every possible problem of disability, three million widows have found no common voice and their many difficulties have been swept into the background.

This might be because women themselves are not yet sufficiently articulate and have been too sheltered in marriage and in the home, and too little concerned in continuing education and training for life in the world. It might also be said that women as a social group have not generally acquired the type of loyalty to each other we can often observe amongst men. Perhaps the competitive search for a desirable mate, followed by the isolation of home life, have made of them unwitting, and sometimes unwilling, loners. It is a price most marriage exacts. There is also a need for a far greater understanding of the social and economic aspects of marriage and widowhood, and for a more compassionate grasp of what bereavement and grief mean to a family.

The work of the Cruse organization for widows and their children, which is mentioned frequently in this book, began in 1959 as a pilot experiment which, as a social worker, I initiated, watched over by a group of professional people who had in various ways observed the effect of widowhood on women. Group counselling and discussion among widows followed a simple pattern and soon showed very clearly the many problems encountered in this experience and the need for support of a special kind. Widows came from all backgrounds, mingling together with the sense of a common experience of some magnitude. The work has grown rapidly as a national counselling service giving expert help to thousands of widows through the years. Where local committees of professional people and social workers could be established, branches have been formed. It has not proved easy to maintain work of this challenging nature, for many wish to put this subject aside, preferring not to be involved in the distress and problems of others.

Through these past years I have been encouraged at all times by a most devoted staff and a growing number of professional people, many of them doctors and many Quakers. Working on a shoe-string, as we have done continuously, there is at last more evidence of interest and support from Trusts and official sources. While acknowledging the generous hospitality of the National Marriage Guidance Council, the London Marriage Guidance Council, the Guild of Health and the Westminster Pastoral Foundation for Central London meetings, the need for a Cruse house of our own is now of paramount importance. My husband, Dr Alfred Torrie, who shared with me so much of the development of Cruse and hoped that it would become a permanent family service in the community, died on 21st April, 1972. Since that time I have myself tested the validity of all our work and its sensitivity to this important experience so many must meet.

In this book a direct approach is made to the widow herself in discussing the various difficulties she may encounter. Certain chapters are necessarily extremely practical, others deal with the emotional and social aspects of widowhood. The book is planned so that the stages of experience can be met at the time of need. Most of what is written will be helpful to social workers, professional people and all those whose calling brings them in touch with widows and their children. Training seminars in the understanding of bereavement and rehabilitation counselling are now a feature of Cruse work. While the confusion of early widowhood is likely to call for support of a personal kind, most widows will find in these pages much that will help and enlighten them. It is in a sense a textbook for them especially. More detailed material they will find in the publications of the Cruse organization.

An important addition to this revised edition of *Begin Again* is the international appendix, which presents a picture of the situation of widows in other countries. Not only will this be helpful to families 'on the move' but it offers a challenging commentary on the statutory and social position of women in today's world.

ACKNOWLEDGMENTS

I wish to thank Mrs Barbara Pentreath for her help in 1973 in updating the first edition of *Begin Again* and collating the material for the international appendix of this edition.

Grateful acknowledgment is due to the following authors and publishers for permission to reprint in this book extracts from works in which they hold copyright:

D. W. Baruch and H. Miller, *Sex in Marriage* (George Allen & Unwin Ltd); Heather Jenner, *The Marriage Book* (Gerald Duckworth & Co. Ltd); Peter Marris, *Widows and their Families* (Routledge & Kegan Paul Ltd); D. W. Winnicott, Address to the Annual General Meeting of Cruse, 1968.

The winter of grief

A Dream
I dreamed I was in a great snow wasteland. The trees were bare and etched starkly. There were no birds and the silence was complete. I was sitting on a tree stump and in front of me was a hole in the ground. Suddenly two old men came towards me carrying a box. They lowered it into the hole and I knew that someone I loved dearly was there. Without looking at me the men turned silently and shambled off. I was utterly desolate weeping there.

A Voice
Your only solace just now is your rose garden. Do you know the difference between snow and black ice? The first is good for the ground, the second kills. Snow is a blanket keeping the earth and the plants warm. It is a fertilizer too when it melts, and before this happens there will be snowdrops and when the sap rises the trees will sprout. The winter of grief is a season only.

1

From marriage to widowhood

Marriage a goal—Growth of progressive attitudes—The 'Great Unmentionable'—Widows' changing image—An egocentric and affluent society—Fear of involvement—The Cruse organization begins its work.

To be happily mated and supported in marriage and motherhood is the dream of most girls. Whatever changes in the pattern of this role may come about, the ideal is still to live in satisfying partnership with the man of your choice, to carry and bring up the children you have conceived together, and to accept what you hope will become the rich years of middle and old age with mutual understanding and love. Mothers themselves, and frequently fathers too, continue to feel that a goal has been reached when daughters leave the home safely for what all hope will be a happy marriage. This is the social pattern still, though nowadays scored about with periods of tension and worry as experiments in relationships and working careers are tried out by both sexes. The parents of today's young mothers and fathers have themselves lived through difficult war years, or their aftermath, when men and women together encountered much emotional stress. During these years, too, women emerged from a life of relative protection, fighting many battles to establish a place for themselves beyond the confines of their homes. In marriage, the divorce laws, the Married Women's Property Act, the enlightened work of the Marriage Guidance Council, and a much more open approach to sexual matters have played an important part.

Children have been nurtured under new child guidance teachings in the society which has, since the war, become progressively more affluent. Their impact as young adults has sometimes seemed to burst homes apart, creating a new social pattern full of unrest. The expressed dissatisfaction of many women with their lot has played its part too. Increasing longevity resulting from better health and medical care has brought its own special problems.

The great technological advances of the last fifty years have widened the horizons of the ordinary man and woman through the immediacy of radio and television and the speed of jet and space flight. By contrast we face the threat of atomic and germ warfare, the violence of the urban community and of racialism, the pollution of our natural environment and the destruction of its life. To say the least, it is an astonishing and confusing world to live in, and certainly one which calls for the partnership of men and women as they face its challenge. For many the safety and protection of marriage are all the more important. Not all are able to match their step to the speed of change, or to be at peace in the clamour of the new age. Some who look on the world with a woman's eyes and have a woman's training may even find the spectacle daunting, if not terrifying. In its wider aspect this is the backcloth against which women must and do experience widowhood today. This is the world in which they must stand alone. To begin a new kind of life is a double challenge just because so much has changed in our environment.

It has been said that our age has killed compassion, that too much has happened to us too fast in the last fifty years, and that political expediency and loud demonstrating are no substitute for deep human understanding. Even the young, in all their agitating, have not often shown a continuing capacity to give and to care to the point of personal loss or hurt. In studying the situation of many widows in Britain today—there are over three million—the first surprise is that we can find so little to guide us on the subject. One could say that its deeper significance and even the weight of its practical problems have only lately been fully realized. Indeed to work in close touch with the bereaved is to discover our present society and its taboos in a new way, and current attitudes to death seem to show that this is both a subject and an experience we do not really wish to explore. It has been called only recently the 'great unmentionable'. Not unnaturally those who come close to the death of others must share in the cloud of fear which has gathered. As in a woman's experience of giving birth, so in death and its nearness we are taken over into a new dimension where few are at home and others have no wish to linger. Understandably, the one who will be most closely affected by death is the widow, whose whole life is likely to be changed. Even the old picture of widowhood with its Dickensian overtones and its Poor Law background has not entirely disappeared: here and there it may have been replaced by that of the Merry Widow. Neither, however, shows us a true picture of widowhood as it is now known in Britain, but both serve rather to project an unfortunate image of a situation which deserves both our compassion and our aid. What is often seen as the social 'failure' of poverty is made worse by the fear of death itself. This should not be allowed to block our understanding of a human situation in which community support is essential.

From time immemorial women have been the spiritual high priestesses attending the great private events of life. They above all have been care-givers in the human family at all stages of its growth and change. If publicly they would sometimes appear to be subordinate to men, privately they have reigned supreme in what has often become a greater awareness and perception of suffering and of joy. For them life has often been uninhibited by intellectual analysis. In this immediacy of experience they have woven a richer tapestry, created a more intricate pattern than have most men. On the periphery of the male jungle they have been protected from its hurts, and only at times of national crisis have they surrendered their ancient role as homelovers and keepers. If sometimes today they appear both ill at ease and bewildered in the man's world in which they must make their way their true state is revealed in bereavement. The death of a husband is in large measure the shattering of a home, as evident as a bomb blast which shears off the front of a house, leaving all its intimate affairs exposed. That men and fathers matter in the modern woman's world is very evident. A man represents in the community not only the stable income and protection of his family, but he forms the main bridge into its life. It is to him that the mother and children look for knowledge, decision-making and for the teaching of male skills. Man's role in the man/woman relationship might cry out for changes, but of its importance few can be in doubt.

Many will say that only part of the picture is here, and that we already have a new type of woman, in most ways free, and in many mistress of herself. Management-conscious and sexually free, she conforms little to the old pattern. Some say that two great wars have brought this about; that a society fighting for its life had no place for the 'little woman' act, and that even today her daughters in their trendy clothes and dolly makeup are really only acting a part. If they have not wholly grasped the nature of their role and have a somewhat inept way about them, this too will change. But what of the large numbers of women who are over fifty-five? Is it true to say that they too have accepted a more modern image for themselves in present-day society? From my work among widows it does not appear to me to be so. Many fit very truly the dictionary description of the widow, where we read that to be widowed is to be 'deprived', 'robbed', 'stripped', 'dispossessed' or 'left destitute', and the very word itself means 'emptiness'.

Should we be entirely surprised if an egocentric and affluent community fails to take such a person to its heart? After all, to do so could prove to be a 'missionary' work of considerable dimensions, and this is not the day of the missionary. Furthermore those reared in British nurseries and schools have a very marked fear of showing emotion. If a woman's personal life is shaken to its foundations, allying oneself with her difficulties may call for a degree of involvement which will threaten both comfort and peace of mind. This may be why so few stay long enough in the circumstances of another's grief to discern and understand its clear pattern.

An experience which exposes family life and personal relationships at their deepest point is a challenging one for relatives and others who come close to the bereaved. 'There but for the grace of God go I' may well be a proper response. Certainly the success of any help given to the bereaved will be measured in the expansion of life and renewed care for her family and for others which the widow subsequently shows. If the family has believed that 'the Englishman's home is his castle' and that people properly 'keep themselves to themselves' the widow must now cut down her hedges and learn a new way of living. If she is to be happy again, retreat and seclusion must end, and she will have to find the way to live with an open door and an extended family. She may find too that she is truly needed in a world where kindness and goodwill are often in short supply.

The work of Cruse over the years has shown that the need for a voluntary service, supported by married men and women and which can be called upon in any county for informed help, is urgent. In the brief surveys which follow it is clear that such support is needed by women of all backgrounds and that it should go beyond such services as are now available from statutory sources.

Of the first five hundred widows who approached the organization for support of various kinds, eighty-two husbands had been professional men, three hundred and sixteen had been skilled workers, and seventy-eight unskilled. Three hundred and twenty-one out of the five hundred widows were between the ages of forty and fifty-nine. A similar number had children varying from one to five in family. The largest number of children was between the ages of eleven and sixteen. Of the five hundred, two hundred and forty-two received the widowed mother's allowance; eighty-six had independent and non-statutory pensions, and eighty-one were receiving supplementary pensions (Social Security); a hundred and fifty-two of the widows were in full-time work, eighty-five in part-time work. Half of the widows owned their own houses or had them on mortgage. One hundred and fourteen were tenants and eighty-four were council tenants.

A further thousand questionnaires have now been analysed and interesting facts have emerged. Out of the thousand, two hundred and ten of the widows were between twenty and thirty-nine; six hundred and thirty-two were between forty and fifty-nine, and a hundred and twenty-nine were sixty or over. Twenty-nine did not give their ages. Fifty per cent came from professional or non-manual and forty per cent from unskilled backgrounds. Three hundred and sixty owned their houses and a hundred and fifty-nine had mortgages. There were a hundred and seventy-two council tenants, a hundred and eighty-six ordinary tenants. Four hundred recorded full or part-time work. The total number of children up to age twenty-one was one thousand one hundred and eighty-two, of whom nine hundred and forty-five belonged to the widows between thirty and forty-nine. A hundred and eighty-seven of the children were under five; three hundred and ninety-two between five and ten; three hundred and twenty-one between eleven and fifteen; and two hundred and eighty-two between sixteen and twenty-one. A hundred and eleven widows received supplementary assistance; a hundred and ninety-four had pensions from their husband's work. Seventy-eight had private savings or income. Ninety-three were receiving compensation or insurance money relating to their husband's death. Out of the one thousand widows forty-five recorded general benevolent fund gifts, nineteen had had gifts from the British Legion and twenty-four from the R.A.F., R.N. and from S.S.A.F.A. together, a total of eighty-eight. A hundred and twenty-five recorded no religious affiliation, five hundred and eighty were Church of England members, eighty-nine Roman Catholics, fifty-nine Methodists, forty-three Presbyterians, fifty-one Congregational and Baptists, and fifty-three various denominations or societies.

Both these surveys reveal that the widowed mother remains an exceedingly vulnerable member of our community. The increase in the number of young widows is seen and in both surveys we note the preponderance of women in middle years with children under ten years of age. The basic need for secure housing is met in house-ownership by a third of the women, but a hundred and fifty-nine had no insurance cover for the mortgage, and have therefore to continue payment on a greatly reduced income. In both cases general maintenance of the house has also to be met.

Active church membership is not generally recorded, but we note the large number of Church of England members and the high proportion of Catholics and Methodists. The small number receiving benevolent fund grants is revealing, and points to inadequate referrals, to lack of information or to narrow terms of reference. As the majority of these widowed mothers are attempting to cover the same overheads formerly met with the husband's salary, their situation in our affluent society offers a greater contrast. The need for an organization of their own to care for their interests is all the more evident.

In the investigation undertaken by Cruse only those able and willing to complete a questionnaire were included and these came from all parts of the country. In local branches a feature of the membership is the considerable number of older and very lonely women. Their problems are covered to some extent in this book, but details of their situation are not included in the surveys mentioned.

The rapid growth of the work among widows has shown clearly the need for a special type of service which can give support without an undue burden of gratitude or the feeling of personal inadequacy associated with much of the *de haut en bas* social service of the past. Courage and independence of spirit must at all cost be kept alive and unimpaired.

I should like finally to turn to all those social workers and others who may find themselves working with the bereaved. To become involved is to ask ourselves how we too have responded to the loss in our own lives and whether that response was sound. In it is the seed of on-going mental and spiritual health or of potential breakdown.

Ruth Draper, in one of her incomparable monologues, speaks of an experience she and her sister had in Ireland shortly after the war. They were travelling in open country and in a heavy downpour of rain found shelter in an isolated cottage. The woman there welcomed them kindly and they sat talking. She said her only son had been killed and she had been broken down by grief. Then one night she had a dream and her boy stood wan and ill at her bedside. When he spoke it was an appeal: 'Give over weeping, mother, or my wounds will never heal.' She said that from that day she stopped grieving and a new serenity became hers. This simple peasant woman had found one of the fundamental secrets of living. If we bind our griefs to us we may find ourselves spiritually and physically bleeding to death. It is imperative that wounds heal, and heal well. There must be a point of acceptance in order that we may go on. This cannot be said lightly. The pain of life may mean much suffering but there is a day to surrender grief. It is when we fail to let it go that we cease to live. Coming to terms with loss requires great courage and acceptance. If, looking back, we lose our way here, we may, like Lot's wife, become no more than the salt of our own tears.

Beginning again is no cliché. It has about it the feel of a new day. And if, stepping out, we stumble here and there, it will not matter because the road is new for us and there are discoveries to make. Our progress will improve as we go. Of one thing we can be certain; we need not find ourselves alone.

Things to do at once

Confusion after a death—Practical ways to help
—Immediate financial needs—A husband's personal file—Circumstances of death—If the
Coroner is called in—The death certificate—The
body for medical research—A husband dies
abroad—The death grant—Burial and cremation regulations—All the people to advise
—Personal effects to dispose of.

A death in the family is a dramatic event and usually relatives rally round to help the bereaved. Only those with no relatives, no people of their own, are left by themselves at such a time, and whatever the strength or weakness of family ties, this is a time when the widow prefers to have her own people round her. The private affairs of the family are likely to be exposed, and she herself will prefer a social situation in which her distress is contained, although her greatest problem may lie in the ineptitude of relatives in dealing with the complicated situation which invariably follows a death.

Correct steps are best taken by those with cool heads, but this is not an open invitation to relatives to make up the widow's mind for her on any major matters. When the miasma of grief has lifted, any wrong decisions taken on her behalf may well cause her great difficulty and unhappiness. In time perhaps there will be greater understanding of the bereaved situation and its aftermath in this country. As things are, the tendency in families most nearly connected with the death is to cover over the matter as soon as possible, but it is useless to create an apparently tidy arrangement of the widow's affairs to the detriment of her future. She herself must, or should, participate closely in all important decisions, so time must be allowed for her emotions to settle. This may by no means suit the relatives. The remark so frequently heard—'Oh, you'll marry again'—is more often an unconscious shelving of responsibility than a true recognition of what lies ahead for the widow. Many have no wish to remarry; having had one successful marriage they are altogether dubious about second attempts. Others, who may long for a return to the married state, find no suitable partner. The old idea that any unmarried woman in a family is something of an embarrassment still persists, whether she is a widow or a spinster, and relatives fear that they may find themselves involved in some way. In spite of the immediate problems it is always in the widow's best interest to treat the future as a time of personal rediscovery and rebuilding. The life ahead is hers.

There are necessary and often harrowing jobs to be done after a death. If it is due to an accident or a suicide, an inquest will follow. In any case the death must be registered and there will be decisions to be taken regarding the disposal of the body and the funeral arrangements. At this time a widow needs the support of a steady hand and quiet reassuring guidance as all practical steps are taken. She is likely to be suffering from shock. She may be greatly confused and agitated. She may be cool and unemotional. Either way someone can give the right help. It is an other-regarding and selfless task of vital importance, whether undertaken by a relative or a social worker. It can also fairly be assumed that this is a job no one likes doing, and hence it is likely to be hurried to its conclusion as quickly as possible.

For the majority of widows grief and an overwhelming feeling of insecurity go together. The first and simplest call for money will remind her that the breadwinner has gone. It is therefore all the more important that steps should be taken to lift this anxiety while she is most deeply upset. A wise husband will have made provision for the payment of a cash sum to meet household expenses in the first weeks after his death. This will allow time for the settling of insurance and pension claims and for the reading of the will. Such an arrangement may release a sum of money while other assets are frozen pending legal settlement. Where this provision has not been made, relatives or the husband's workmates or firm may put a sum at the widow's disposal as a gift or for later repayment. If there is nothing now the husband's wages have ceased, the Social Security officer should be asked to call. The vital thing is to lift the widow's immediate financial anxiety and to communicate a feeling of support to both her and the children. Such matters as pocket money for the children and the regular meeting of their school expenses must be considered as part of the total situation. At the end of this chapter we deal briefly with the widow's pension position, but it can be said here that if the widow can be temporarily sheltered from the cold blast of the regulations it will be a kindness. Those staying with her can obtain the necessary forms for her.

One of the most trying first acts for a widow is the finding of personal papers relating to her husband. Some men keep their documents in an orderly manner, others do not, and there may be difficulty. A mind confused and shocked is not the best to employ in a long-drawn-out search for papers. If these documents have been assembled in a personal file and have been lodged with the bank manager or family solicitor it will save much distress. In another chapter I give a memorandum which every husband could usefully leave with his wife or a friend in case of emergency, a small act which could mean a great deal at an extremely difficult time. It has been known that a superstitious attitude towards death may prevent a husband from taking thoughtful action of this kind, but it is possible that a timely word will help some husbands to overcome their fears.

Those who are not too shocked or exhausted by long nursing will undoubtedly wish to take some of the practical jobs into their own hands. There are certain steps which must immediately be taken and which will precede the funeral, although arrangements for this will be under discussion early. The Consumers' Association publishes a useful leaflet called 'Arranging a Funeral', and they have a booklet, 'What to do when someone dies'. Social workers may wish to have these booklets and family members may find them useful in the emergency.

Death must be registered within five days of the event. It is usually a very painful experience for a widow to have to do this herself, and every effort should be made to save her from having to do so. The person doing the registration must take the deceased's medical card and the medical certificate. He or she must also have the following information;

1. Date and place of death.
2. Full name and usual address of deceased.
3. Correct age and occupation.

4. If married, date and duration of the marriage.
5. National Insurance card.
6. National Insurance or war disability pension book if this applies.
7. Details of any other pension.

The Registrar then issues the death certificate, which costs 25p at the time of registration but 40p if applied for later. It is wise to get at least two copies.

CORONER'S PROCEDURE

There are some widows who are greatly troubled by the circumstances of their husband's death and it is important to know that the law makes it the duty of the Registrar to report certain cases to the Coroner and defines the circumstances which govern this duty as follows:

1. Where the deceased was not attended during his last illness by a registered medical practitioner;
2. If the Registrar has been unable to obtain delivery of a duly completed medical certificate of the cause of death;
3. Where it appears to the Registrar from the particulars contained in the medical certificate, or otherwise, that the deceased was not seen by any certified practitioner either after death or within fourteen days before death;
4. Where the cause of death appears to be unknown;
5. If the Registrar has reason to believe that the death was unnatural or directly, or indirectly, caused by any sort of accident, violence, or neglect, or was attended by suspicious circumstances; it is the practice for any death occurring within a year of a fracture to be reported;
6. Where death occurred after an operation necessitated by injury, or under an operation, or before recovery from the effects of anaesthetic;
7. If it appears to the Registrar from the contents of any medical certificate that the death was due to abortion, industrial disease, or poisoning (including industrial or food poisoning), or

circumstances of military service which may have accelerated or caused death.

In addition the law also provides that certain persons have a statutory duty to inform the Coroner of a death. These are:

1. The Governor of a prison; whenever a death occurs in any sort of H.M. Prisons, the Coroner must hold a full inquest.
2. The person in charge of a mental hospital must report the death of any certified mental patient to the Coroner.
3. He must also be informed of the death of any temporary patient who dies in an unregistered hospital or in a nursing home. In the latter case the duty lies with the doctor who attended the patient during his last illness.

THE HUSBAND LEAVES HIS BODY
FOR MEDICAL RESEARCH

If the husband has left instruction for his body to be given to medical research before being buried or cremated there is a procedure to follow. It should, however, be pointed out that the executors or next of kin may decide against this wish since no one can legally own a body once it is dead and a bequest of this kind is therefore not legally enforceable. On the other hand, unless it has been specifically said that the husband does not want this to happen the executors and next of kin can give the body for medical purposes after death if they wish. It is obvious, therefore, that anyone who feels strongly about this should give his or her directions. The steps to take are these: the professor of anatomy at the nearest university medical school, or the Inspector of Anatomy at the Department of Health (in Scotland at the Scottish Home and Health Department) should be approached. He will send a form which can be placed in the testator's personal file. If the deceased had taken this step the executor or relative completes and sends in the form after the death, together with a special medical certificate which the doctor will complete. Offers of bequests are not usually accepted from people under the age of fifty, because their life expectancy is at least twenty years more, during which time they might move away or change their mind. No guarantee is given that a body will be accepted.

Those who have never dealt with a funeral may be astonished at the cost. It will greatly exceed the Statutory Death Grant of £30

(1973), usually by at least £50, and the more that is made of the event, the higher the figure will rise. If the family member who is advising the widow can possibly do so he or she should encourage her to choose a less elaborate funeral for which she can reasonably hope to pay. Failing this, any debt will prove a serious embarrassment to her at a time when her troubles are many. Funeral customs vary, but the widow's wishes may be taken into account according to her means. If there is a private funeral insurance this should be taken up at once. Should the widow wish to entertain after the funeral she will certainly be glad of any help in the practical arrangements. There will probably be relatives with her for meals and some staying overnight.

The undertaker's estimate should make clear whether or not funeral costs include graveyard plot, surround and headstone with inscription, or, in the case of cremation, the disposal arrangements of the ashes. A widow will be thankful for someone to watch over these matters with the greatest care. There have been tragic cases of funeral debts of £80 to £250, where the sum was mainly for graveyard plots, and such heavy debts may necessitate a complete overhaul in the family finances beyond that already suffered. Undertakers have been known to prosecute widows, and threatening letters can be a source of great anxiety. In such a case a social worker may be able to arrange for bills to be met on instalments within the widow's means. It is sometimes easier for somebody not involved in the family's affairs to do this. Fees for cremation vary from £6 to about £13 and more formalities are required. The cost of a church service will be additional to the undertaker's bill. Everyone is entitled to be buried in the churchyard of the parish in which he had his home, whether or not he died there or was a Christian. A burial fee of about £3·50 is normally charged. Separate permission and fee are required for a headstone.

If the husband dies in hospital the Medical Social Worker will advise about the procedure.

A HUSBAND DIES ABROAD

The death of a British subject abroad has to be registered according to local regulations. It helps to register the death with the British consul in that country as copies of the death certificate may then be obtained later from the Registrar General at Somerset House.

If the body is brought back to Britain the Customs will want to see a certificate of death or an authorization for the removal of the body from the country of death. Before cremation a doctor's certificate stating the cause of death has to be sent to the Home Office, Romney House, Marsham Street, London SW1P 3DY, so that a cremation authorization can be issued by them.

If death occurred in Scotland or Northern Ireland, but the funeral is to take place in England, the death certificate issued there will be accepted as evidence of death.

THE DEATH GRANT

This is a statutory payment, normally of £30 (1973), based on contributions and is payable to the person responsible for meeting the cost of the funeral expenses. A grant to pay the actual cost of the funeral is paid if the death occurred as a result of war disability or during hospital treatment for it. This grant is adjusted in respect of any National Insurance death grant. The claim for the death grant should be made as soon as possible and must be made within six months of death or it may be lost. The Registrar will issue a special death certificate free of charge for National Insurance purposes. If the widow or her representative cannot call at the local Social Security office, she should complete parts A and B on the back of the special certificate and send it in by post. Claim forms will then be sent to her.

Should the husband die overseas, in some circumstances the death grant may be paid. If the widow is herself abroad at the time she should write to the Overseas Group, Department of Health and Social Security, Newcastle upon Tyne. The following papers will be necessary in all cases:

The death certificate
The husband's National Insurance contribution card
His birth and marriage certificates
The Family Allowance or Social Security order books issued to him or the widow
The undertaker's estimate or bill for the funeral.

14

It should be noted that the death grant is not liable for estate duty.

SUICIDE

There are many suicides every year in this country and it is helpful to have correct information in this distressing event. Doubts are sometimes expressed about the right of the person to Christian burial. Suicide is no longer regarded as a criminal offence under the law, and such persons may therefore have Christian burial, although the clergyman officiating could confidentially be given the details.

GETTING THINGS STRAIGHT

It may be helpful to remind the widow's family of the various practical steps which should be taken in dealing with the personal affairs of the bereaved. There are, for example, certain people who must be informed.

1. The employer and trade union   The husband's employer and his trade union must be told. The name and address of the union branch secretary are on the card, but if this cannot be found the address of the trade union can be found in the telephone book. Some trade unions have special benefit schemes to which the husband may have contributed. Such notification is especially important if death has occurred as a result of an accident at work or through a scheduled industrial disease. All trade unions have lawyers specializing in compensation claims and make no charge for dealing with the cases of deceased members, including taking legal action where necessary. Compensation law is highly complicated and the most expert help is to be found in trade union legal departments. This does not contradict the advice given below about obtaining help from a local solicitor, as long as he knows the compensation claim is being handled by the trade union.

2. The bank   As we have said, some men arrange in their wills that a certain sum of money will be immediately available for their widows' use. Failing this, a widow may find all assets frozen and be obliged to open an overdraft in her own name, pending a settlement of her husband's affairs. If the husband and wife had a shared bank account this situation will not arise, as she may then draw in her own right. In either case it is most important that the widow should know how she stands. If there is no joint account the bank will automatically stop payment of standing orders and any cheques presented after notification of the death will be returned marked 'drawer deceased'.

Where debts are due for payment they must be shown as such in the Inland Revenue affidavit and will be paid by the executor or administrator after the grant of probate has been obtained. The bank should be consulted regarding cheques, dividend warrants, etc., payable to the husband. The Trustee Department of the bank, even if not appointed as executors in the will, can be asked to assist if the relatives wish it. Bank charges for handling an estate vary according to its size and complexity in the same way as solicitors' charges.

3. *The family solicitor*   If there is none, it may be advisable to put the widow's affairs into the hands of a reputable solicitor immediately, but much will depend on her capacity to understand her affairs. She may value discussion regarding her plans but resent any attempt to make up her mind for her. In the majority of cases, the widow is well advised to avoid too many radical decisions on her affairs while she is still disturbed by the shock of bereavement. Many have lived to regret hasty decisions made following the persuasion of over-zealous advisers and relatives. For many, any suggestion of legal help will give rise to anxiety about the fees. This should be discussed with the solicitor. His charges are based on the size of the estate and are therefore nominal in a small one. If the widow wishes it the solicitor may be asked to come to the house. If property is involved, his services will almost certainly be required in arranging transfer into the new ownership after probate has been granted. He will also tell her of all the documents she will have to produce—e.g. Post Office savings book, bank statements, post-war credit certificates (*see* page 17), tenancy agreement, hire purchase agreements, etc., and details of any known debts.

Anyone deciding to handle the estate personally should apply to the Personal Application Department, Principal Probate Registry, Bush House, Aldwych, W.C.2, or the district registries in the main towns. In Scotland 'confirmation' (the equivalent of probate) is obtained. If the widow herself or one of the executors is able to deal with such matters, expense can be saved in this way, but if the estate is likely to give rise to complications advice should be sought. An arrangement to see a solicitor under Legal Aid can be made to obtain advice for the widow, but he cannot settle her affairs for her. It should be noted that in some aspects the laws relating to disposal of property under a will, and to intestacy, are different in Scotland from England and Wales.

4. The insurance company If the deceased was insured, notification should be sent to the head office or to the local agent of the company. If a solicitor has been engaged he will deal with this. The insurance policy should not be handed to anybody other than the solicitor or a representative of the company, who must produce evidence of identity. If sent by post the policy must of course be registered.

5. Inland Revenue and P.A.Y.E. Since P.A.Y.E. is calculated over a year's income assessment, it may well be that a widow is entitled to some repayment on her husband's current year's tax. The Inland Revenue office must be informed of the husband's death so that adjustments may be made. Claims can be submitted within six years of the year of assessment. Such money may be invaluable to the widow in the first year of financial difficulties.

6. Post-war credits These have already been cashed by most people. If not, or if the certificates had been mislaid and the claimant put to the back of the queue, now is the time to claim. A widow may claim her husband's, on his death, as well as any due to her in her own right. The amount they are worth appears on the certificates, and the Inspector of Taxes will give their value for Estate Duty purposes. Application forms can be obtained from any post office.

7. Department of Health and Social Security The local Social Security office should be informed immediately. A relative, friend or social worker can do this, asking for the forms to be sent for claiming death grant, widow's pension, etc. There is no need for the widow to go to the office herself. If there are complications the local office will usually send someone to the house.

8. *The landlord*   If the husband has arranged joint tenancy with his wife of a rented property, many difficulties will be avoided. If the rent book is in his name the widow must immediately arrange to transfer the tenancy in order to ensure security of tenure for herself and her family. There are still many tenancies where the transfer of tenancy remains the statutory right, but many properties were decontrolled by the 1957 Act. If there is already a statutory tenancy and this has passed from the original contractual tenant, the widow may well have no security of tenure. Even if a widow is uncertain about her future she should be advised to take the step to get security of tenure where she is while she decides what to do. She should not, however, sign a fresh tenancy agreement or accept alternative accommodation without first consulting her solicitor or the Citizens' Advice Bureau, otherwise she may find that she has unwittingly forfeited statutory protection as a tenant. If she is in a council house the local housing manager should be informed of the bereavement: she may find that under her new income she is entitled to rent and rate rebates.

9. *The building society*   The building society or other mortgagor should be informed of her husband's death and, if necessary, the company may be approached regarding suspension of payment until the affairs are settled. If the widow is remaining in the house she may ask for a lower rate of mortgage repayment to meet her new circumstances. The period of repayment will then be extended. It is a disturbing fact that so few couples who arrange a mortgage for house purchase safeguard the completion of the payments in the event of the husband's death. It costs very little to take out an additional mortgage protection policy, or, if the house is being bought with an endowment mortgage, the entire debt is paid by the insurance company if the house-owner dies.

10. *Social Security supplementary benefit*   If the husband died intestate it may well be that the widow finds herself with practically no money with which to carry on. The Social Security office should immediately be advised and the officer will call to make

appropriate arrangements. If the family is already receiving Social Security assistance the office must in any case be advised of the death.

11. Hire purchase firms The position should be clarified as soon as possible. Some H.P. agreements have provision in them for cancelling the debt on the death of the purchaser. No rush should be made to part with H.P. goods until the terms of the agreement and entitlement are quite clear.

12. Husband's clubs Every organization to which the husband belongs should be advised. A friend or relative can well do this.

13. The children's schools It is most important that the headmaster or headmistress of the children's schools should be advised of the death of the father: they will then be in a position to consider ways of helping the widow if necessary, will advise her regarding bursaries, grants for clothing, free dinners, travelling expenses and will keep an understanding watch over the children.

14. The husband's personal belongings Widows will differ in their feelings about this matter. Some will wish to keep everything, others to part with painful reminders of the past. Whatever decision is taken the sense of loss still has to be faced. It is probably a mistake to make any changes or removals immediately, especially if there are children. The evidence of their father's late presence is important while they adjust to his loss. Practical decisions such as the disposal of clothes may be a matter in which friends or relatives can help. These can be parcelled up and sent to Oxfam, given to the British Legion, to 'New Bridge' or 'Circle Trust', to Toc H, to the W.R.V.S., Church Army or other local organizations. All will be glad of them for men in need. If the husband was a craftsman and there are tools to be disposed of, these should be priced by an expert so that a fair figure is obtained. Toc H men will sometimes help in this, as will men in the British Legion. Art equipment can be sold through the local further education centre. Other specialist equipment can be placed through the appropriate body. Very great care should be taken over the sale of any machinery, of cars, bicycles, caravans, boats, etc. Unfortunately, cases of sharp practice and gross meanness where widows are concerned are by no means uncommon. Protection at this vulnerable time is most important. Cruse headquarters will advise if the widow does not know whom to approach. The great thing is to lock up equipment safely until there is time to go into the matter of sale with care.

3

You start from what's left

Every man should make a will—How to make a family guide—A widow's will—Small estates —Estate duty—Property in joint names —Children and guardianship—Intestacy and the widow's rights—Codicils—Gifts and trusts —Protection by insurance—The state pension position—Supplementary benefits.

The reading of a will can be an occasion of much family tension. It is done after the funeral and usually by a solicitor with all the family present. Unfortunately many men are hesitant about making their wills until too late, to the great inconvenience and sometimes distress of their families. We offer here practical suggestions to enable a husband or widow to arrange their affairs in an orderly way for their dependants. This document can be kept in the husband's or widow's personal file and left with the bank or with the executor, and a copy in another place. In this chapter we give brief details of the situation which intestacy can bring about, quite apart from the possibility that the person who has died will not have his or her wishes met in the disposal of the estate. We include also a brief reference to the state pension position and supplementary benefits, for in a very true sense these can be the financial basis of the widow's new life.

HELPING THE EXECUTOR OR RELATIVE A FAMILY GUIDE

If the husband (or widow) makes several copies of the document bearing the following information, much trouble will be saved:

My will is with..
The copy of the will is with ....
(Addresses and names)
My bankers are ....
(Address)

My solicitors are ....
(Address)
At this date I own the following property (investment in stocks
and shares, bonds etc.) ....
My share certificates are deposited with..................................
. ...
My insurance policies are ....
I own freeholds ....
    Leaseholds ....
The deeds of the properties are at ....
Mortgages are ....
Dates of birth of self and children..
Married at...
To...
My home is at ....
My business is at ....

Date: Signature:

(Add further details of any valuables, loans, etc.)

Anyone over eighteen, and every widow, should make a will,
for this ensures relative simplicity in dealing with personal property. The testator (the maker of the will) appoints an executor (or
more than one) to distribute his or her properties. A relation or
friend may accept the task. In some cases a solicitor, bank or insurance company has been appointed executor and the Trustee
Department of the bank will help to wind up the estate. The department also handles the buying and selling of stocks and shares
for the normal percentage. In other cases the family solicitor has
both drawn up the will and is named as executor. The Public
Trustee Department, which used to accept the role of Trustee, is
now being wound up.

A WIDOW'S WILL

A widow with considerable property will usually have a family
solicitor to help her draw up her will. If she owns only her house
and/or its contents or small capital, she is advised to note carefully who is to have what, before seeing her solicitors. It will
shorten the interview if she knows her mind. A will form can be

22

bought at the stationer's, and the instructions re signing and witnessing must be carefully followed. A witness must not be a beneficiary. If a widow has no relatives she may leave her effects to a charity. Most annual reports of charitable organizations (including Cruse) print a form of bequest as a guide to put in the will. Any legacy left to children where the age of inheritance is a factor should be held for them by the executors.

PROBATE

A will must be proved before the executors may carry out its provisions. After duties and fees are paid, the Probate Registry issue the probate with a copy of the will attached.

INTESTACY

When a man dies without making a will he leaves many problems to worry the family. Usually the affairs cannot be settled so quickly, and the widow may be in great difficulty in this period. A solicitor will require a search to be made before intestacy is accepted and Letters of Administration can be granted. Finally, a widow whose husband dies intestate will be required to find two guarantors who will stand surety for the estate in perpetuity against the possibility of a will ever being discovered leaving the property elsewhere. It is possible to take out an insurance policy against this eventuality and for this only one premium of a few pounds is required.

ESTATE DUTY

Possessions must be declared, and the Inland Revenue may require their valuation for estate duty. This includes furniture and possessions which may have been regarded as part of the joint home. There is no joint ownership in law as a rule, and articles belong to the person who bought them or to whom they were given. There is no duty on estates under £15,000 (1974) and in addition property devolving upon the deceased's widow is exempt from duty up to a limit of £15,000. An estate exceeding £15,000 pays Estate Duty at an increasing percentage. If a life interest only is given to a wife, then no duty is payable when it passes to the children. If the property is given absolutely, Estate Duty is payable by the wife and again when she dies. If the husband dies on active service, or as a result of illness so contracted, the estate may be exempt from duty. This must be checked with the Estate Duty Officer.

PROPERTY IN JOINT NAMES

1. Houses   The advantage of houses held in equal shares in the joint names of husband and wife is that on the death of the husband, provided joint ownership has been in existence for at least five years, Estate Duty is payable only on the husband's share. The house will be assessed considerably below its market price (since only half of it belonged to the deceased) and Estate Duty starts being assessed at £30,000 with all other assets taken into account. If the widow inherits the whole property and then dies herself within a year the estate is protected by Quick Succession Relief from double death duties.

2. Investments   The disadvantage of investments in the joint names of husband and wife is that on the death of the husband Estate Duty is often payable on the whole.

CHILDREN AND GUARDIANSHIP

A parent with children under eighteen should by will appoint a guardian or guardians. Each parent may appoint their own and indicate that the surviving parent is to act with the guardian. This is a very important decision for a widow who finds herself in sole care of the children, as also for the children should anything happen to her. In the latter case, and if the widow has made no provision for guardianship in her will, the local authority's Children's Department must be told, and will assume responsibility for the child or children. Usually the Children's Officer tries to find foster parents or keep the child in one of the local authority's children's homes. If at all possible children of the same family are kept together. In arranging guardianship for their children widows can often find some difficulty. It is important to discuss this matter with the solicitor, the bank manager or any organization of a beneficent kind, which makes a practice of taking care of the orphaned children of its employees or those who are its members. The widow is well advised to get this matter straightened out, for many have considerable anxiety about their health and the position of their children should they themselves die. If there are relatives who can take care of the

24

children, some understanding should be arrived at so this is clearly accepted.

The statutory Guardian's Allowance is £4.90 (1974) per child per week, and can be applied for by anyone who takes into his family an orphaned child provided he contributes more than anyone else to the upkeep of the child. The allowance must be claimed within three months of the child joining the family. Family allowance cannot be paid as well for the same child. Where the widow remarries there is a good deal to be said for the new husband adopting her children legally if they are small. The whole matter, however, needs to be discussed with care, as the widow's children by her first husband have a right to their father's name and may resent its being changed. They are, after all, his children. Once the second husband has made the decision to adopt, he then takes on the same responsibility for the children as he might for any he already has, or who will later be born of the marriage. They would then all share the same name. For the purposes of the statutory family allowance the whole family would now be treated as one.

DESTRUCTION OF OR DISPUTE REGARDING WILLS

Destruction of the will by mistake or in a fit of temper does not revoke a will, and a copy of the will can be proved. Where it is desired to dispute a will on the ground of insanity or fraud or undue influence, a caveat can be entered through a solicitor at any Probate Register. It lasts for six months and during that period any attempt to prove a will will result in notice being given to the person entering the caveat. It should be pointed out that it is very difficult to dispute a will and prove the facts to upset it or a gift in it.

OPERATION OF THE WILL

The will takes effect as from the time of the testator's death. Therefore, if by his will the testator leaves a house or other specified property to a particular person, and then sells or gives that house or property to some other person, the person whom he intended to benefit will not get the house or other property. Moreover, a person may leave all his property to X, thinking it is worth only £500, and when he dies thirty years later it may turn out that it is worth £5,000. X will, however, take all the property because the will has not been altered. It is therefore desirable to look at one's will and reconsider it every year.

CODICILS

A codicil to a will is really a short will additional to the original one, altering some of its provisions. It must be executed in the same form in all respects as if it were a will. If the whole will is to be altered it is better to make a new one. If more than two codicils are required it is also better to make a new will.

TRUSTS

If a trust is created by a will so that a surviving partner gets the income for life and has no power to dispose of capital, estate duty is payable only on the death of the person making the will and not again on the same property on the surviving partner's death. If the property is given absolutely to the surviving partner, estate duty is payable a second time. If the trustees of the will are given wide powers of investment and the surviving partner is appointed trustee with other persons there are few disadvantages in disposing of property in this way. A life trust is not advisable if the surviving partner will have to some extent to live on capital, although the will can state that capital sums may be loaned to the wife which need not be repaid till her death.

GIFTS

Gifts made to charity at least one year before death are exempt from duty. However, since March 1972 duty is only payable on the excess of charitable gifts over £50,000. Other gifts are liable for duty unless made more than seven years before death (although if the donor dies at any time within the fifth year after making the gift, the value of the gift is, for estate duty purposes, reduced by 15 per cent; within the sixth year it is reduced by 30 per cent; and within the seventh year it is reduced by 60 per cent). Marriage Settlement gifts by a parent or grandparent, or by one spouse to the other, are excepted as to the first £5,000 (or £1,000 if made by any other person). Gifts regarded as part of the deceased's reasonable normal expenditure, and gifts not exceeding £100 to any one person (in certain circumstances £500) are also excepted (1973).*

* See Addenda, page 185.

Under the Married Women's Property Act, 1882, section 2, a policy of insurance can be taken out by a husband or wife on his or her life and expressed to be for the benefit of the surviving partner or the children or both. This creates a trust in favour of the persons named and, while such policy is not exempt from duty, it pays duty as an estate by itself. This will normally mean that it will pay a much lower estate duty. The general rule is that all the property passing on a death is added together and the rate of estate duty chargeable is fixed by the total value of all the property. This does not apply to policies under the Married Women's Property Act. This is why the rate of duty may be very much lower. The premiums payable can be spread over as short a period as five years and the policy can be made fully paid up after three annual premiums.

THE WIDOW'S RIGHT TO ACQUIRE THE HOME

A man may die without having made a will, leaving his wife living in a house or flat. She can then compel the administrators to transfer the property, including any land, to her as part of her share in the estate. Where a will has been made this provision does not apply to a widow whose only interest is in income, that is a life interest, unless the husband has required a capital sum to be paid in discharge of the life interest. Moreover it does not apply to leases or tenancy agreements due to expire within two years from the death or which can be terminated by notice from the landlord within those two years. It does not therefore apply to most rent-controlled property. The widow should notify the administrators by registered post of her intention to exercise, or not to exercise, this option or she may require the administrators to have the residence valued before deciding.

The decision to exercise the option once notified to the administrators in writing may not be revoked or altered without the administrators' consent. Where the value of the house exceeds the value of the widow's interest in the total estate she may still take the house and make a cash payment of the difference between the two values.

THE STATUTORY PENSION

It would probably be true to say that very few men are aware of the details of the statutory pension which for many widows must become basic income. For some it can prove to be all they have to live on. The regulations governing the pension position are somewhat intricate and both relatives and the widow herself may find them hard to follow. A set of leaflets may be obtained from the Department of Health and Social Security who will also help in interpreting them. The booklet 'Caring for the Widow' and the Pensions Fact Sheet published by Cruse may also be helpful. What matters is that the widow and her family should be quite sure that they are receiving their correct allowances as either civil, industrial or war widows, with or without dependants.

There is not space in this book to detail the provisions, but attention can be drawn to a few points. In the first place it is generally accepted that no person may be in receipt of more than one payment from a statutory source, but at the same time it is worth noting that if a widow is claiming from two sources, either under the National Insurance Act or from some other statutory fund, she will usually find that payment she receives will be restricted to an amount equal to the greater of the two benefits. Another important point is that while deficient contributions lead to a reduction in payments, any increase of benefit payable for a child is always at the standing rate.*

POSTHUMOUS AND ILLEGITIMATE BABIES OF WIDOWS

As quite a number of widows bear their husband's child after his death, it should be noted that after the first twenty-six weeks of widowhood she is entitled to receive the widowed mother's allowance for the remainder of the pregnancy. The necessary claim form for the maternity grant should be obtained from her local child welfare clinic and there should be no delay in putting in the claim.

In the case of a widow who has had no children previously and now bears one illegitimately, the title to widowed mother's allowance cannot arise because the child was not in the late husband's family at the date of death. She may now claim supplementary benefit to cover the child which will be granted to the extent necessary to bring her income up to the level at which her requirements, including those of her child, are assessed under the Ministry of Social Security Act. Children are normally accepted as dependent for supplementary benefit purposes up to the age of sixteen, and if

* See International Appendix.

they continue in full-time education beyond that age they may be accepted as dependent. Otherwise at the age of sixteen they may claim in their own right, although this necessitates registering for employment at the same time. Once the child reaches the age of sixteen and starts working, the mother, who during the dependency years has received her special provision through the Social Security Act, will now cease to receive this and will be expected to work if she is fit and under fifty. Age-related widow's pension is now payable from the age of forty and the full Widow's Pension (which is the same as the standard retirement pension) if she is aged fifty or more when her husband dies. It should be remembered that the guardian's allowance is not available for illegitimate children, for this is intended only as an orphan's benefit.

In cases where a widow has been living with a man without marriage and ceases to cohabit, she can apply to her local Social Security office for the reinstatement of her widowed mother's allowance if she has dependent children by her husband, and she should do this without delay. If there have been illegitimate children born of the later union they cannot be taken into account in determining her title to widowed mother's allowance at any time, nor can an increase of this allowance be paid for any illegitimate children. The illegitimate children can, however, be included in her family for family allowance purposes and she should make a claim on form FAM. 12.

Although a widow who is cohabiting is not entitled to widow's benefit, she can claim increase of benefit for her children, including those who are illegitimate, if she becomes entitled to sickness or unemployment benefit by virtue of contributions she has paid herself. If she ceases to cohabit but decides to continue to pay contributions she may claim increase of benefit for illegitimate children if she becomes sick or unemployed.

HOSPITAL IN-PATIENTS

After a period of eight weeks in hospital under the National Health Service, a widow's benefit or retirement pension is reduced. The amount of this reduction will vary according to the rate at which benefit is normally payable, whether or not the widow has a dependant, and the length of time she continues to need hospital care. Her earnings-related supplementary allowance, however, is not affected.

If a widow remarries (or lives with a man as his wife), she ceases to be entitled to any widow's benefit from her previous marriage. If, however, she is entitled to a retirement pension she will not lose it if she marries again when over sixty. An industrial widow's pension will cease if the widow remarries, but she will receive a gratuity equal to one year's pension. A similar gratuity may be paid on remarriage to a war widow, or, if the husband was an officer, no gratuity is paid but the pension may be restored if she again becomes a widow.

WIDOWS OF MIXED MARRIAGES

Widows of mixed marriages who are living in this country, such as refugees, Commonwealth immigrants or aliens, are likely to have special problems and they are well advised to keep before them the address of the International Social Service of Great Britain. In some instances a widow married to a British subject but not herself originally British, and whose husband did not qualify her for a pension on his contributions, may successfully apply to her original country for a pension in her own right. If she is able to get such an application supported by a well-known citizen in her country of birth her claim will undoubtedly be helped.

RETIREMENT

It is important that widows reaching the age of sixty should understand the meaning of retirement as understood by the statutory authority if they do not intend to give up paid work at that age. By carrying on with regular work and continuing to pay contributions a widow can earn a bigger eventual pension, but she must give up for the time being her retirement or widow's pension. At the age of sixty-five she can draw retirement pension in full even if still working regularly. If she decides to claim retirement pension at sixty, or at any time between sixty and sixty-five, she can earn up to £13 a week before the earning rule applies. Her retirement pension will not be reduced below the level of widow's standard pension (£10 a week, 1974).

Widows can, if they wish, have their retirement pensions paid to them quarterly or monthly in arrears by crossed draft. This may suit some women better than collecting the money every week at

the Post Office. A pensioner who cannot attend the Post Office
owing to some disability can authorize another person to draw the
pension on her behalf.

SUPPLEMENTARY BENEFITS UNDER THE MINISTRY
OF SOCIAL SECURITY ACT

Supplementary benefit is an extremely important provision in this
country. It operates as a 'safety net' to give help to all those citizens who fall into temporary or continuing financial need which is
not completely met by other statutory pensions and allowances.
The year 1948 happily saw the end of the Poor Law social cover,
when it was replaced by the National Assistance Board. In 1966
this was again replaced by the Supplementary Benefits Commission within the Ministry of Social Security. The benefits administered by the Supplementary Benefits Commission are
supplementary pensions for those of pensionable age (over sixty
in the case of women) and supplementary allowances for those
under pension age. The purpose of both benefits is to bring a
person's weekly income up to the level laid down under the Ministry of Social Security Act.

If a widow thinks she may be entitled to supplementary benefit
she should at once make a claim by completing form SP. 1 if she is
over pension age or form S. 1 if she is under pension age. Both
these forms, which include a guide telling more about the scheme,
can be obtained from any Post Office or local Department of
Health and Social Security office. An officer of the Supplementary Benefits Commission will then come and see the
claimant in order to get the necessary information about her
circumstances. If she is over pension age she may choose, if she
prefers, to attend at the Department of Health and Social Security office instead of being visited.

Supplementary pensions and allowances are usually paid by
books of orders cashed at the post office. Younger widows without dependants may, however, be required to register at the Employment Exchange as a condition of receiving supplementary
allowance if they are fit for work. In that case the supplementary
allowance will be paid at the Employment Exchange together
with any unemployment benefit payable.

A young person over the age of sixteen years who is still at
school will be treated as a dependant of the widow if she is

31

receiving supplementary benefit. Immediately on leaving school, and if without work, the widow's child must register with the labour exchange in order to qualify for Supplementary Benefit in his or her own right (whether or not his mother is receiving Benefit) in the event of remaining unemployed or becoming sick.

If a widow is in receipt of supplementary pension or allowance or on an otherwise derived very low income she may claim on behalf of herself or her children exemption from payment of prescription charges and a refund of any charges incurred under the National Health Service for spectacles, dentures or dental treatment.

A widow who is not satisfied with the decision made on her supplementary benefit claim has a right of appeal to an independent Appeal Tribunal.

A useful booklet published by the Citizens' Rights Office (1 Macklin Street, London WC2 5NH) is the National Welfare Benefits Handbook. It covers Supplementary Benefits, the 'Wage Stop', the cohabitation rule and welfare and housing benefits.

4

The conflict of emotion

Taking the shock—Society's taboo on feeling—Men, women and children respond differently—How the widow feels—Dependency—Loneliness in grief—Envy and anger—Seeking oblivion—Relatives and friends—So many difficulties—The body cries out—Hope the best medicine.

Widowhood is for many a subject too painful to contemplate. To men it spells the possibility of death, even their own death, to women it is a threat to all that means home and marriage. Many women will remember the dramatic moment when an 'Any Questions?' team was asked what each feared most—a highly revealing question if the speakers were to be honest in their answers. The only woman on the team was very well known. She hesitated a moment, then said: 'I fear most becoming a widow.' It seemed as though an iceberg had turned over.

'I never believed this could happen to me. My husband was not perfect but we suited each other. The day before he died we were laughing and joking together. There was nothing to warn me.' 'My husband was so young and we were on holiday with the children. He died of a coronary in the street, right in front of us.' 'We had made all our plans for the new house, even the deeds were signed, then it happened.' 'They came from the hospital to tell me —a policeman . . .' These widows express simply the immediate shock of death. For others the experience may come after the husband's long-drawn-out illness, perhaps with much pain. Sometimes the family is isolated in its concentration on the one who is ill and the death makes an unbelievable gap in the home life and its nursing routine. Of course many dangerous illnesses can now be controlled by new drugs, but there remain those which require an exhausting period of nursing. When this situation has preceded a death the widow has often been so preoccupied in carrying the load that there is little inclination or energy to think ahead. Then suddenly the tension ceases and she is alone and no longer needed. She becomes aware that all the 'keeping up' of the nursing period has left her completely drained of strength and nervous energy. The commonly held belief that long illness prepares the family for the patient's end is often not in keeping with experience. The dependent invalid is missed as though he were a loved child. Nevertheless sudden death through coronaries, accidents or suicide means a special shock to a family, even if they are spared the experience of witnessing long illness, physical deterioration and its accompanying dependence. In a younger person, too, so much is left unspoken and unfinished, which holds its special grief for those who must go on. Where the marriage for any reason has been unhappy, the widow may have very confused and distressing feelings, but she will share with others the same loss of status and all the practical difficulties.

In his book *Death, Grief and Mourning* Geoffrey Gorer gives figures showing that only half of the widows were present at their husbands' deaths: many, it seems, die alone in hospital. Inevitably, at such a time, the immediate dependants are closest to the experience and for them there is grief to overcome and a new life for which they must prepare. There may be heartrending situations which will play their part in the subsequent experience of mourning. Each death must be assimilated and understood by those who are nearest. Many widows reject the idea of death and go through a period of hearing the husband's key in the lock and all the other sounds of his normal activities as if they were still happening. It takes time to believe that death has taken place.

Into this deeply private experience comes the conditioning of social behaviour patterns: 'keeping up', 'being brave', 'taking it in your stride', 'keeping a stiff upper lip'—we have all met these well worn phrases, perhaps even used them ourselves. They are the constricting patterns of response expected in our taboo-ridden society. The laurels are for those who create least embarrassment and who will put a time limit on their grief. 'Weep and you weep alone' is still a very true and British saying.

Unhappily, to be widowed is often to enter the dark world of other people's fear. Death and tragedy, after all, are always for the other person, never for oneself or for those nearest to one. Perhaps understandably those at the periphery of the experience transfer their fears to the widow, thus adding to her distress. It is almost as if some lurking superstition exists suggesting that death is catching. The Japanese say a widow is a 'woman waiting for death'. How else to see her empty future? Even the wearing of mourning bears its tribute to the habits of primitive societies where the bereaved gashed themselves and wore rags so that the spirit of death should not return, recognize them and take them too. Our materialist age has little room for mystery and the passing of life is, after all, an experience beyond our intellectual grasp. It can and must be accepted. One who was alive in body and could communicate with us, and whose life was part of ours, has suddenly gone. There are no more answers, no human and moving touch. A warm, responding person has become a shell. Death appears to be a final rejection.

Grief and loss are interwoven and are part of the deep response of all human beings to this experience. The end has come and nothing more can be done. The French say 'every parting is a little death', but the physical finality of death can test the very depths of personal philosophy and courage. To see too the difference between the responses of men, women or children in the family is to be aware of the role each plays in the home pattern and the society around them.

There was a time, not so long ago, when men in this country could weep publicly and not be discredited. Were they to do this today they must run the risk of being thought mawkish and unmanly. Why and exactly when little boys were first taught that it was important to hide emotion is an interesting speculation. Perhaps it was all bound up with encouraging pluck at 'taking a toss' or biting the lip to hide the pain of kicks and bruises suffered by the sportsman or the child in the rough life of the playing field or the street. Soldiering has never had any room for softness either, and the concept of courage has often been confused with the handsome appearance of the man in uniform which women have always admired. Often the women themselves were over-protected and, although fearing what life could do to their sons and lovers who marched away, did not realize that they might well have encouraged an emotional barbarism in place of the acceptance of natural feeling which could give their men depth, understanding and sensitivity. Undoubtedly the training-out of emotional response leaves tensions which can give rise to considerable stress in events which call up emotion. Many of the physical heart conditions so familiar today may in fact be related to this failure in our men to deal with feeling. An even more unfortunate response in sensitive children can be the growth of sadistic and masochistic patterns of thought and behaviour.

Considering the impact of loss on women we know that in Britain today there is far less show of feeling than in other countries of Europe. The black-robed widow of Italy, France and Spain is accepted as rightfully set apart in mourning. In England both the mourning and demonstration of feeling are 'out of fashion'. Of course, to some extent this attitude is part of the nursery pattern which has been used in the upbringing of boys and which, in some degree, has been transferred to girls. In the rough lingo of the streets both sexes can be mercilessly teased for tears. For children this form of toughening is mainly used against physical hurt: there is no preparation for the loss of a parent or other types of bereavement. Here we have to look deeper into parent/child dependence to measure the effect of the experience. Nowadays, however great the shock and disruption of home life, there is little outward show once the funeral is over. The family is expected to get back to normal quickly. The rejection of grief by the people around her often makes it harder for the widow to deal with the depth of her emotion and its confusion. Society's response could almost be said to underline the teaching of the nursery about cuts and bruises.

Death is no respecter of persons. It comes to high and low in the land, and the women and children of a man's family vary in the special behaviour patterns they have learned and on which they must take the impact of the experience. A woman's social position, her secondary role in marriage, the 'little woman' act, or the tough sporting role where womanly feeling is often a disadvantage, all belong to the varied background in which most British women have been conditioned. The woman with a straightforward response to grief will probably emerge best, and in a reasonable time, from the experience of bereavement.

With men the funeral is the end of a harrowing experience. They feel too that it should also be the end so far as the public are concerned. To grieve outwardly is unmanly and, in any case, you should not 'wear your heart on your sleeve'. There is something in the quick and continuing movement of life which says, 'the king is dead—long live the king'.

In children, response may well be more complex because the experience of loss is new and there is usually little to prepare them. Where they are directly involved and have been taught a pattern of emotional restraint it may well be bewildering if the parent appears out of control. The widow who sends her children away while she struggles for self-mastery often exemplifies this response to upbringing. The mother always in control is the image she has set for herself. It may be that those who have found treasure in their emotional lives and have kept their natural warmth will be more able to hold the impact of loss and have something over for their children. Those who have studied the various responses to grief have often encountered the 'brave' woman who is praised for her lack of demonstration and cool sense of purpose as she deals with her family and practical decisions. The emotional turmoil is rejected or is sent underground. Unfortunately, this type of response has its comeback. Unresolved grief may prove to be a bomb which can unexpectedly explode in later years, often when another loss is experienced.

So confused can people be at this time that those unfamiliar with the emotions aroused by death can handle the situation badly. It helps to know how common such turbulence is, and informed compassion will support the bereaved with truer understanding. There are physical and emotional symptoms to be recognized too: 'I had butterflies in the tummy'; 'I would have been quite unsafe driving the car—my concentration had gone'; 'I took all the things to lay and light a fire and then didn't know what I was there for'; 'I could not eat and didn't want to drink'; 'I longed to sleep in oblivion but lay tossing with my mind tirelessly turning things over'; 'I was panic-stricken, dry-mouthed, wondering how I could pay my way alone'; 'I wanted desperately to be alone and then immediately longed to be with others'; 'I wanted to talk and talk—anything—the words just tumbled out'; 'I felt no one knew my experience—I was silent inside'; 'I was furious with the smugness of those around me and I was often unbelievably rude'; 'I wanted to throw my arms round any comforting man just to feel his security—I didn't want sex, I wanted a father's love, but men don't understand'; 'I longed to cry and cry but no tears would come'; 'I was numb and cold inside—even the children who ran to me meant nothing—I had nothing to give'; 'I don't think I really believed it was true. It was just a nightmare and I would wake up'; 'They wanted to take his body to the mortuary but I wouldn't let them. I kept vigil all night and somehow the fact of his death reached deep down'; 'I kept telling myself it was a mercy to have the pain ended but I still could not accept it'; 'I moved in a strange dream world where everything was different and I had no measure for the dimension of things'; 'It was so quiet—I had never known anything like it'; 'He had known his death was coming and had prepared all the practical things for me so that I knew just what to do. There was none of that terrible confusion. I felt the warmth of his love for me in all he had done'; 'Anger kept boiling up in me —how could he go and leave me to face all this?'

In these bare comments we catch the feeling of those who have encountered one of the biggest experiences any of us may know. The impact of bereavement is powerful and goes deep. It is as though it opens up all the wounds of life we have known. An experience akin to an earthquake is likely to tumble what seemed secure and to reveal fissures previously covered. Personality defences are common to us all and how we deal with attacks upon them depends on many things. Grief is not an illness, but if our handling in childhood has been austere or over-protective, the loss of a loved and supporting person may have far-reaching effects. These can cause the bereaved to react with aggression towards others or against the self; in a clinging to others or a withdrawal from them; in a see-saw of feeling which is withdrawing and clinging by turns; in a constant demand for help from those with special knowledge; in punishment of others thought to have caused the death, even to the point of 'going to law'; in withdrawal from those thought to be persecuting the bereaved and in a total blaming of and withdrawal from what is seen as 'God'.

Of these reactions to grief some appear more puzzling than others, and if the bereaved have no one of understanding to whom they can turn the symptoms can be very distressing. 'I thought I was going round the bend' is a common remark, often followed after reassurance by 'what a relief to know these feelings are quite usual'. To have lost a greatly loved partner and then to feel waves of anger against him seems strange, and yet this is the natural response of a child where dependence is a big part of relationship, and the parent figure has gone away. Much in marriage shares this type of dependence. The bereaved person with an over-developed neurotic conscience, often deliberately inculcated in children, has a permanently unattainable ideal of behaviour and is unable to direct any negative feeling towards the dead partner. All the blame is turned back on the self in waves of guilt and condemnation. The anger is swallowed but not digested. There may be suicidal feelings—'Life is no longer worth living'. There is masochism and a self-torture which can go on and on. Fortunately when balance is restored this self-accusation will be lifted and the bereaved can abandon her hold on the lost partner without in any way rejecting him. Memories then become simply a storehouse of treasure belonging to the past. Such acceptance recognizes that all life experience is built into what we are now and in that sense can never be lost. Even the discovery of a new love cannot alter this, but serves rather to enrich it.

One of the most difficult aspects of bereavement is its loneliness. We may no longer follow the customs which enjoined seclusion, but the fragmentation of family life today, with its few children, can leave the widow very much alone. In a large and busy Victorian household wholly given up to home pursuits, there would usually be more than one resident woman who could be turned to for sympathy. Nowadays the house is probably empty, and the children at school or moved away. Everyone is busy and there is no time for long exchanges. This factor needs to be borne in mind by social workers and clergy who may come into the widow's experience. At this time it is the understanding of women above all that is needed. While widows may want to lean on a father figure it is often only in another woman that they can find the depth and breadth of understanding they most want at this time. It can be that such help is best given by those who are not part of the family.

Compared with a good marriage, widowhood is a great impoverishment and very understandably it can cause envy and jealousy of those not so deprived. One widow refused to use the front rooms of her house because she could see couples walking by. Another felt black envy every time she saw a car with father driving the family. Others felt jealous of their children's sex lives even if their friends' marriages did not stir them. Any apparent unfairness in statutory regulations which gives a better deal to married women can become a very sore point too. Unfortunately such discoveries are usually made in the first year of widowhood as the widow struggles to find her feet.

It is said that 'time heals' and, while this is in a measure true, it reminds us that there are many types of scar. Some have a permanent weakness and may break down again, some are ugly and obvious, others may be neat and almost imperceptible as healing continues. We believe that loving and imaginative support given immediately on bereavement will lessen the effect of loss, where withdrawal by the family, friends and society around deepens and worsens the experience. Nature is kind in giving a temporary covering of emotional anaesthesia, when feeling seems to go, but many have found that after this period the real awakening is all the more painful. It is at this time that caring by others matters very much indeed.

However much delaying tactics are advocated, there are important decisions the widow must make quite soon and this further serves to underline the loss of her partner's support. Women vary in their recovery rate and some will be confused and anxious to the point of panic for a considerable time. Many seek oblivion in drugs, some in drink. Sleepless nights may become a habit. Those who are accustomed to working amongst widows have discerned a common pattern in most homes where the husband has died. According to the closeness of family ties and the number of supporting relatives, attention is given to the widow over the first six weeks. The impression is gathered that she should be able to manage her affairs once advice of various kinds has been proffered. Unhappily in some instances relatives may gather only for the reading of the will. The relationship of the widow to her in-laws may be poor, and once the son is gone interest in his wife may wane. The clergy may call after the funeral and then not come again. Neighbours may give continuing help or shrink from the possibility of involvement. Friends may prove to be no more than acquaintances when the test comes. The fortunate family will find steady, warm-hearted and patient support through all the difficult months of the first year and even after that the widow and her children will be welcome in married homes. Much depends on the past social life, the family set-up and the nature of the community around. A great deal too will depend on the widow's responses. She may so fear pity that she rejects genuine friendship. She may have temperamental outbursts of anger or weeping which her family and friends dislike. In a true sense she may sometimes feel she is 'beside herself' and strange company for those whose patience and understanding are in short supply.

It is usual for many widows to be discouraged, depressed and deeply unhappy. Everything seems to come at once in the early months and the first year can seem to offer blow after blow. Financial worries are legion, there are endless forms to deal with, the will takes time to settle, the statutory pension position may come as a grave shock. Where there are children the burden of their dependence may often seem intolerable with no wages to meet the bills and, coupled with this anxiety, there are often difficulties in behaviour and control to handle as well. Housing is a major and immediate concern as most widows find that their income has dropped to less than a quarter of what the husband provided. Much the same overheads must, nevertheless, be met. Getting work, while it may seem the obvious course, is frequently extremely difficult and for many concentration on other matters beyond the home situation is for some time impossible. Add to these problems a lack of knowledge of the statutory and voluntary services and of where to go for what, and the shattering blow which the husband's death has dealt can be more clearly seen.

As many doctors know, this is a time when physical symptoms can crop up too, and most widows admit that for a year or two they may be in indifferent health. The stress encountered in emotional and practical spheres prints its inevitable pattern on the body. It is not uncommon for widows to complain of more than one of the following symptoms, although fortunately these may pass off as adjustment to the new life comes: backache, rheumatism, arthritis, headache, asthma, skin trouble, loss of hair, palpitations, tenseness, irregular or total suppression of periods, poor sleep, loss of weight. Understandably many women make more calls at the surgery than usual. Their doctors do their best to help, often giving them sedatives and sleeping pills, while they know that hope is the best cure for the deprived and unhappy and that wounds heal when the weeping stops. It has been said too that 'there are some things that are only seen by eyes that have wept'.

As you emerge from this difficult period, when so much thinking and feeling are confused, you will gradually see yourself more clearly. You will know now that some of your sorrow has been mixed with a very real fear of the future and what it holds for you.

The early period of exhaustion when everything in your mind and body seems slowed down will have passed and you will have come to terms with brooding, knowing it now to be the way to despair and the exhaustion of your reserves. You will have caught yourself getting into what some have called 'the suffering habit' and learned to reverse the process. By avoiding the most hurting memories you can give yourself more time to heal and in this the very ordinariness of life and its routine will help. The days when you worked yourself to a standstill in a feverish attempt to forget will be over, and very slowly you will become aware of progress. While above all you do not want to be hurried you can see now that you have discovered nature's time limit on grieving and it really doesn't matter whether it takes one or two years for you to feel a person you can respect and live with and on whom others can rely again.

5

Towards a new beginning

The first two years are a bigger challenge than many realize—Nothing morbid in self-examination—Blaming God and feeling guilty —A new reason for living—Giving people the benefit of the doubt—New relationships and ones to watch—Morale building—Hope and healing are on your side.

To experience widowhood and to make a success of your changed life after many years of marriage is a much bigger achievement than most people realize. Lack of a loved male companion, the comfort of his physical nearness, the loneliness, financial hardship, the total responsibility, the breakthrough to the outside world in relationship and in work—these all must be faced with courage, persistence and endurance. Indeed this experience seems to take all you have got in sustained effort and often you dare not look far ahead. As someone put it, 'the future has no face'. But you find too that you need courage only for the day and this can be yours. You have learned what your stress-taking capacity really is and may have been surprised at how you 'kept up' in the early days—you were admired for your 'bravery' even though there were times when you were alone, feeling utterly lost and frightened. It is not easy to feel so tossed about and bewildered—so 'not yourself'. You have heard about women who say they felt buoyed up with strength and others who felt their husbands near, but so often for you everything seems bare and empty with only an echo of a loved voice going far, far away. You find that there is nothing constant about the emotions of bereavement except the pain which must be borne.

Of course you have met those who say, 'Don't join up with widows—they will only depress you', but, in what is largely uncharted country for you, to talk with those who know the road is strangely reassuring. Here are some of the things they say: 'I found I was incredibly confused and my mind seemed to be in a whirl'; 'I was always tired and hardly had energy to get through the day'; 'I felt I was cliff-hanging but I had to work and that kept me sane'; 'I had thought I was made of better stuff and never believed anything could so upset my balance'; 'It all seemed to go on and on, not the grief, that was there like a dull pain, but the pushing oneself to do things'; 'I felt quite unprepared to meet all this. No one seems to talk about it or understand it'; 'My home had always meant so much. There no longer seemed any reason for anything, so why bother to keep up standards'; 'I let myself go. I had always dressed and kept nice for my husband. Without him there seemed no point'; 'I had no feeling. It was like being an automaton'; 'It took me quite a time to get through this confused period'; 'I felt I wanted once for all to understand about my husband's death and why it happened, but no one likes talking about death'; 'Religion and philosophy had never mattered to us in our marriage, which was very happy, but now I want some reason for going on. What is it all about?'

In Cruse meetings these matters are talked about freely and sometimes discussion goes deep. The encounter with death and loss stirs up questions which we may never have thought seriously about before. 'I slept badly for months and used to wake panic-stricken at times'; 'I couldn't face the loneliness of the night and took sleeping pills to knock me out'; 'I was afraid to form the habit and tried all sorts of things to induce sleep'; 'For a time I was so afraid of the night that I used to stay up and fall asleep in a chair'; 'I began to think about the meaning of life and whether death really was the end'; 'My husband never talked about this sort of thing'; 'I didn't feel morbid or pious—I just wanted to know'; 'I was angry about my husband's death—he was so alive'; 'I got worried about things that were said about heaven and hell and punishment'; 'If God is love it is hard to see how the death of someone you love fits in'; 'I told the children he had gone to be with Jesus but I had no idea what it meant—just words it seemed'. Everyone was different and yet curiously the same in their experience. Some seemed to find equilibrium more quickly than others. Beyond the confusion were those who held out the hope that there was a new freedom to find, and that it was possible to discover yourself as a person in a new way. Some found a reason for living in a new devotion to their church and peace and strength in awakened faith; others felt a tide of anger in themselves and allied themselves with causes new to them, and there were those who got through the dark because a hand was held out to steady them.

At such a time it seems natural to wonder what we have depended upon apart from human strength and love. It is almost as though a husband can be invested by us with some kind of godlike quality so that through the years, and often quite imperceptibly, more and more of our personal burden of living and belief has been laid upon him. During marriage we may have allowed our own beliefs to fade away and there has been no expansion into a new understanding. In need and in grief we can find that the God of our childhood is too small for the scale of this experience. We may run to the Church we have not visited for so long and find a 'doll's house' lit with candles, or an austere building full of history's echoes. When heaven within us has died away we may make the most important discovery of all, that we have no spiritual roots from which to draw the strength we need.

Touching bottom is both an experience of devastation and a new beginning. You feel now that nothing worse can happen to you and in a strange way this opens your eyes to new possibilities. What greater challenge could you have than to face the life in front of you alone in your own strength? It is as though you were offered the raw material for making something all of your own, and because you are an adult and not a child the challenge stirs you in a special way. 'I was afraid, but stimulated. With a little help and encouragement I felt I could make something of my future and felt too that my husband would have wished for my success.' But personal responses can be very different and the urgent need to find a source of strength is there often. Courage is not there all the time and there are black days when you may even want to give up.

In one of his books Stanley Jones tells of his travels in the Himalayas and of how one day he watched an eagle battling against a storm. He saw that it was caught in the violence of the wind and being blown against the rocks. Then suddenly it appeared to change the set of its great wings so that it could fly with the power of the storm instead of fighting a losing battle against it. In human tragedy and the suffering it brings there is an echo of this experience. Each of us, in our own way, must find a source of strength to enable us to live through it and even to turn it to good. Mercifully there is a time limit on true grief, and many have found that after a time the new ways are established and a new strength has been found.

You will often be thankful for the practical matters which demand your attention. There are so many things now you need to know. You may feel especially ignorant about dealing with officials as the seemingly endless decisions which face you must now all be taken on your own. Women who go out to work seem to know more and be more sure of themselves, and sometimes you will be tempted to feel that your time of responsibility for your family in the home does not count for much. Indeed the position you are in can leave you feeling very bewildered. In the beginning you probably had relatives with you, you may have had attentive neighbours, your bank manager and your doctor may be most helpful; but it isn't enough. The time is coming when you have to understand basic things and learn to look after your own interests. Every bit of knowledge will help towards putting you on your feet as an independent and self-reliant person. The sooner your children feel you can cope, the better too.

Making do on your new income is going to be one of your first problems but, worrying as this may be, life for you does not begin and end in these teasing and seemingly insoluble money sums. There is a new field to conquer—that of relation to other people in your new role. It is good to get this right from the start. What kind of person have you been in your marriage and are you going to continue that way? Warm-hearted and generous with a loving husband and a family income behind you, how will you be without them? Fortunately there is no market value on a warm heart. It is a rich endowment and beyond price. If you forget this and let 'the freeze' set in, life will shrink beyond the loss of a husband and it is you who will be the main loser. So the determination to remain a warm and giving person is important to you. You have to reject the 'double think' which slams the door on goodwill and kindness by calling it 'pity'. You might even remember that it has been said that 'Pity is akin to love'. 'In the early days of my widowhood I made up my mind not to become a "no-saying" person. If people asked for my help I did my best to give it. If they wanted me to go out with them or wanted me to see them I didn't refuse. It was not always easy, but somehow this bridged over the bad times and I didn't get caught up thinking no one wanted me and feeling sorry for myself.'

One of the difficult experiences of the widowed mother is the deadening of feeling in the first months. The children seem to need more, and not less, of your love and the well is dry. 'I just went on the same way, giving the outward signs of love and affection and the practical care, and after a time I began to feel again.' And relatives, on the whole, are kind; but the exposed feeling can be worse with neighbours and casual acquaintances. There is nothing for it but to keep up a good outward show and believe in the sympathy of others. 'I realized soon that many of my married friends were terrified that the same might happen to them. This seemed to account for some of their funny reactions. They were not really thinking of me but of themselves going through my experience.' The best people to help are often those who have been hurt badly. They may not talk so much, they let you talk, and they feel with you without swamping you. Of course, if the experience is recent and the other has not herself recovered you may not be much good to each other. One needs to be just that bit ahead in experience to help someone who is going through it. In your relations with others, some enjoy being 'leant on', but this wants watching, or suddenly you find you have become too dependent and have lost your freedom of decision and action.

Relationships can be different in your new position as a widow and only you can get them in proportion. If you find it hard to stand alone, you will cling on to the first available prop, and that can end badly. So, on the whole, although friendships are precious at this time, understanding based on common experience may be even better. A stable woman friend may be a wiser safety-valve than a sympathetic man friend who encourages you to weep on his shoulder and with whom you soon find you are embarrassingly involved. In all probability he will be a married man, but divorce and the break-up of his own home are not really in his mind. You may find that he is quite prepared to run two relationships, but is not at all happy about your having other men friends. If you have young children you may feel very unprotected as such a relationship develops and you must so often be in the home to look after them. In such circumstances the value of your friendship with other women and even the companionship of one in your home may give you the help you need. Remember too that, however compassionate people may be in early widowhood, the advent of the 'gentleman friend' in your environment may turn your neighbours sour overnight. Unhappily it is usually the widow who is blamed if a relationship with a married man is exposed. It will not be much good looking for fair comment either. A widow has just got to accept the fact that freedom and discretion are going to matter to her in her new life. Even daughters may feel less secure in a fatherless home and situations can easily arise where the widowed mother feels she cannot control a relationship which has developed. If her husband were there matters would be different. So difficulties can grow imperceptibly sometimes as the readjustment in your home and to the community goes on.

Many widows are finding that belonging to a known national organization like Cruse gives them a special kind of support. It can be a 'port of call' if things of any kind get difficult. Around you there will be plenty of people ready with superficial talk and remedies. Their favourite comments are: 'Oh, you will get married again'; 'Join a mixed club'; or 'Don't join a women's group'. Such words offer no practical solution and shut doors on positive and worth-while friendships. Most women who have lived in the protection of marriage for many years find it very hard to move out into the world without their natural escort. As an older woman you find that success in friendship with men will depend a good deal on sharing interests, and in a later chapter I discuss some of the new relationships that can be developed in training and in work for others.

Whether your role is that of the solo widow or of the widowed mother, you will feel better when you have succeeded in bolstering up your 'public image' in a way that satisfies and strengthens you. Once you have made up your mind that you are not going to let go, being a woman you are likely to choose a practical approach to the matter. The impression you create and how you look is going to be important, and you need to remember that, while you may look at yourself rarely, others must look at you throughout the day, whether they are your children, the tradespeople, your neighbour or your workmates. So, without falsifying your feelings, don't make it too hard for them. Here of course you are liable to feel panic about money but, while you are picking yourself up, keep your morale going too, and use what you can to cheer the environment without startling your friends.

As things improve for you you will also find that worry about money lessens and you will acquire the know-how about personal care without undue expense. Don't bother if people say this is superficial. In a world where outward signs have a high priority, and those who weep are expected to weep alone, you are wise to try to look as attractive as possible. If money can be found or spared have a 'facial', a Turkish bath, or a hair-do. If you can't afford, or don't want, any of these morale supports, at least have your hair well cut and groomed. If you let yourself go a lot will go with you. If everything is too difficult get a friend or relative to come in and fuss over you. If you are one of those determined to wear mourning, remember it is depressing for other people unless you smarten it up with white, pearls or modern jewellery. Black is becoming to the happy, and to you if your complexion is clear and bright. One point in this appearance business: don't go to extremes with home tints that hit the eye and garish colours that kill rather than comfort. Be a pleasing-to-look-at widow even when you are sad. When you start planning you will have to budget for clothes, hair and make-up and all sorts of economies can be thought out. Many a widow has said that money spent on face and hair has been more important to her than expenditure on clothes. What matters, after all, is that you step out into your new life with as good a morale as you can build for yourself. Hope and healing are on your side even if it does not always feel that way.

6

Budgeting on short commons

Marking time over decisions—A short-term budget—Learning to foot the bill—All sorts of economies—Selling your unusable assets —Food, shelter and clothing—Cutting kitchen bills—Clothing costs for the family—Bulk and mail-order buying—Taking students—Children cost money—'Secondary' priorities—Taking care of yourself is an economy—Private medical insurance—Joining a widows' organization —Problems of investment.

There can be so much confusion in the family after the main breadwinner goes that uninformed and often unwise decisions may be made. From much discussion with widows it is clear that nothing should be hurried or changed too quickly at this time, a point I have already emphasized. Here I should like to go further into the whole business of making ends meet. This will present a quite different problem to the widowed mother with dependent children, and to the widow who now finds herself alone.

First of all it may be some time before the will is finally settled. Its contents are known, but what assets your husband had may not immediately be clear. Neither the bank manager nor the solicitor will have the full facts to give you at once. Budgeting then presents two aspects: the immediate position, and what you will have for the next six months. Only later will you know what budget you will have to work to. The main difficulty is that in the first six months you will face considerable cuts as well as the strain of taking over completely the reins of management, to which you may not be accustomed. It is a tremendous challenge to health and to all that makes up personal stability. Observing many widows going through this test I have become conscious of the fortitude and endurance which appear to be built into women as a sex. Nevertheless, just as we are not born equal but come into the world with differing degrees of susceptibility to strain, it is clear that help at some points may mean a lot.

Those of you who have been accustomed to thrifty management of a limited family budget must bear with me if occasionally I appear to be stating the obvious. Not all wives are good managers, and the degree of ability you have in the limited field of housekeeping is going to make a lot of difference to the way you deal with the total budget. To become a widow is often to discover a quite different world, more challenging in many ways than women dependent in marriage and motherhood might realize. As a widow you will find that battles of all kinds must be fought. Inevitably many of these will relate to money.

If you are a widow on your own the immediate need is to mark time so that you may decide on your future when you are ready. However sad you are feeling now, you certainly have a future, but it will not drop into your lap like a plum; it will have to be worked for.

Coming down to hard facts, for six months you will have a 'staying' income from your statutory widow's allowance, and an allowance for any children. After that time, if you are over forty or a widowed mother, you will go onto the statutory pension (if your husband's contributions were in order). If your husband was in receipt of a statutory pension for you both, you will go straight onto widow's pension without the extra allowed to others for the six months following bereavement. If you have no other income you should study the Social Security particulars to see if and how you qualify for a supplementary allowance. It is wiser to seek extra provision from state sources rather than use up capital which cannot be replaced. Watch too to see whether any alterations in the statutory provision are publicized in the press. Remember that whatever happens you are better without debts of any kind.

YOUR FOOD BUDGET

You will probably find it helpful to make notes, starting perhaps with a simple test of priorities. First you must eat; you must have a roof over your head; and you need to be clothed. If you are now by yourself you will think afresh about what you like to eat and your menus may be different from those planned for a man. But even if you seem to have lost your appetite temporarily you must cook proper meals and maintain a healthy basic diet with proteins

51

(eggs, cheese, herring, mackerel, or other fish, and meat). You need daily fresh vegetables and fruit, to have milk with drinks, and to keep a watch on fats, sugar, flour and cereals. Unhappy people sometimes eat as a substitute for comfort, and then get more miserable still when they expand out of their clothes and cannot afford new ones. A week or two watching shopping costs and you will be able to see how much it costs to feed yourself. This may be a reasonably modest sum if you are on your own. If you have a family you will already know that food bills can be heavy. Children from the age of fourteen eat one and a half times as much as an adult, and this is likely to continue so for some years. It is not wise to fill them with a tremendous amount of carbohydrate. This may be an easy way to deal with appetite, but it will put up their weight, do no good to their health, and complicate clothing problems. It is better to economize by making greater use of eggs and cheese, for example, in place of expensive cuts of meat.

Bulk buying of groceries and household commodities can offer a very considerable saving if there are children, and perhaps boarders. 'Cash and carry' firms, as they are called, will supply on a bulk buying scheme any trader, group or organization, for cash payment and immediate collection. Such buying can be arranged, for example, through a local Cruse Club if the widow is a member. Most counties and their principal towns and cities have these stores and, with a little planning over orders and an available car for the collection, the buying can be simple. For more individual budget buying other than groceries, there are well-advertised personal shopping service organizations which give free credit with no deposit and send goods on approval with no charge for packing, posting or carriage. Usually there is a comprehensive catalogue and buyers must be householders. Among firms offering discount trade are Better Buying, C.G.A., John Dron Ltd and F.P. Baker & Co. A word of warning here: resist the temptation to order more, or more expensive, goods than you can afford, or you will find the potential saving more than swallowed up, and possibly incur an embarrassing debt.

Of course it is necessary for those who are doing bulk shopping of perishable goods to have a refrigerator, and if you do not already have one, or have to replace an existing one, you should look into the question of buying a reconditioned one. This can be wiser than hire purchase, which can greatly increase the original price of the article. In any case consider carefully which model will best meet your requirements. Those who live near a big town where there is a market will know that prices can vary from one end to the other, and also that on Saturday evenings there are first-rate bargains at shops selling perishable goods. Meat bought ready packed and weighed may be a better buy than that priced by the butcher. It is helpful to have a list showing when such things as fruit, vegetables and eggs are cheapest, so that you can preserve and bottle; a well-stocked store cupboard is a great asset for a family. Since there will be additional calls on your time if you have a family you may find it more convenient to buy certain vegetables frozen rather than fresh, and at some times of year it is also more economical to do so, especially since there is no waste with such goods.

Those who have been used to cooking and shopping on a generous housekeeping allowance will find cookery books written with their new situation in mind a great help. I suggest you contact the Good Housekeeping Institute for a list of their up to date booklets. See also the appendix book list for Chapter 5.

Apart from the fact that the writers of these have the smaller income in mind, use of new recipes will give your cooking a 'new look', which may even revive a jaded interest in the subject. The fact sheets produced by Cruse—'Meat Economies' and 'Building Your Family's Health on a Low Income'—are most useful.

MAIL ORDER

Mail-order buying has become quite a feature of home life in many areas but it certainly has its dangers. It is important to be sure that you are dealing with a reputable firm who will allow you to send back the goods and receive your money again if you are not satisfied. This arrangement is usually recorded somewhere in the advertisement, and you should most certainly look for it. If you run into trouble over phoney advertisements write to the Advertising Standards Authority and report your difficulty to the newspaper in which you saw the advertisement, giving full particulars. Doorstep selling is also something that should be watched and the widow—indeed any housewife—should deal only with the representative of a well-known firm or a person who has been known in the district for some time. You should also be sure that you have the address from which the seller comes.

If at any time goods which you have not ordered are delivered and followed by a demand for payment do not allow yourself to be coerced into buying them. Provided that you do not use the goods it is the sender's responsibility to collect them. If necessary, take a high-handed attitude and threaten to charge storage if the goods are not removed.

Prices of goods at shops which offer trading stamps should be checked carefully as the value of the stamps may be swallowed up in inferior quality of non-branded goods.

HOUSEHOLD EXPENSES

I deal at some length in the next chapter with house maintenance overheads and some of the possibilities for making your home a source of income. Here I will merely note that, unless you are in full freehold ownership of your house, rent or mortgage repayments as well as rates will inevitably loom large in your weekly or monthly budget. If you are in a council house or flat you may succeed in getting a reduced rent. Should you have an uncompleted mortgage and wish to remain in the same house, repayment must continue. This is better than rent, as in the end the house will be yours. In your new financial position your building society may be willing to arrange for you to pay off by lower instalments over a longer period if you wish. You can apply for a rate rebate under your new situation; your own Local Authority will give you details. Comprehensive insurance will probably remain the same. Expenditure on heat and light cannot be greatly reduced unless you are alone and using fewer rooms, but economies can be made by keeping a stricter eye on waste of heat, including hot water. The water rate too will remain the same, with the possible saving of the hose rate if you formerly paid this.

CLOTHES

An important part of your budget is clothing and linen replacement. You may possibly feel that for the time being you have all you need, and do not have to budget for this expense at once.

One of the first decisions will be whether or not you want to go into black. If you do, you will have a considerable expense and know that in a year you will be only too glad to see the last of it and then have to replace everything (most charitable organizations are frequently given black clothes). Even 'the little black dress' will

54

have lost its fashion charm for you, useful as it is. Of course there are widows who are really extremely hard up and in genuine need of certain garments. Here your best plan may well be to get a letter of introduction either from your Citizens' Advice Bureau or from headquarters of Cruse so that you may have a W.R.V.S. allocation from your nearest depot. If you are shy about going to the W.R.V.S. in your own area it can sometimes be arranged for you to go to another district for the allocation. You are allowed six garments twice a year for yourself and for each member of the family. The clothes can be new or nearly new, and the major items are your best economy. Many women have not only had a tremendous amount of fun at local jumble sales, which they help to run for good causes, but they have also found remarkable bargains there with good selection.

Nowadays there are also many 'Nearly New' shops which have been started to assist the funds of various good works. The Y.W.C.A. and Oxfam sponsor these shops throughout the country. They are often haunted by students looking for bargains, and are especially valuable to widows with teenage daughters. These shops can be wonderful also for buying unusual presents which can then be decked out in new boxes and wrappings.

Many widows may find, if they have young children, that they need to make use of their home dressmaking abilities. This can be a very profitable and interesting activity, and can also lead to new friendships if groups get together for the purpose of sharing patterns and learning from one another. Most local further education institutes run dressmaking courses for very low fees which, unless you are very skilled, it would be advantageous to join. For some this leads on to a course in soft furnishing, enabling them to renew such items as curtains, cushions and loose covers which would otherwise be beyond their pocket.

Regarding the fashion side of clothing, everything depends on how much the widow can reasonably hope to afford for clothes she buys 'off the peg'. Many widows with children have to cut down their spending on clothes tremendously and continue to use garments bought years before, making perhaps clever alterations to them. In the first place the basic need is to keep your figure trim: if you let your figure go to seed you are going to have far more difficulty in keeping smart. This then comes even before the buying of foundation garments. You cannot afford a lot of new outfits to cover unnecessary bulges, and even foundation garments of the more expensive kind can have only a comparatively short life. The all-important general decision is to keep to a 'classic' line in your choice of tweeds and woollens and well-cut clothes so that they will last without becoming rapidly outmoded. Attractive stockings and really good shoes will help to keep you in the picture while other women are chasing some, probably unbecoming, temporary fashion. There are excellent shoe dyes now, which for 40p or less can renew a favourite pair of shoes. You can lengthen the life of your walking shoes by sticking on a thin rubber sole as soon as you buy them. The hem line of coats and dresses can, of course, be dealt with at home.

Economizing though you are, at least know your most becoming colours and wear them in hat or scarf. These can be a small expense and lift a quiet outfit into significance. Well-fitting slacks and jeans will save your better clothes from wear as you work at home, and the more expensive 'chunky knit' will probably outlast several cheap ones. A jersey in small man's size bought at Marks & Spencer, C. & A., Littlewoods, Milletts, the British Home Stores, or some similar shop, will look very good and wear well. The harder type of wool will often last longer than the soft wool which rubs into 'pills', for, although a stiff brush will clear them, it gradually removes the body of the wool as well. White, natural and black woollens are useful and can be brightened with current fashion gimmicks usually available for under 50p. If you have never worn costume jewellery this is a good time to enjoy yourself. Jerseys in light colours need frequent washing, but a cheerful shade, provided you can wear it with more than one outfit, will probably do more for you. If you buy a cheap skirt which you like for its fit and colour, line it and you will more than double its life. Always keep a little material from cut-off hems for emergency mending and never throw out good buttons and buckles. On the whole it is not a good idea to keep many garments you do not like and which serve only to remind you of your monetary troubles. Better a small wardrobe of well-chosen clothes of the best quality you can afford, than a rag-bag of items that bore and depress you and everyone else. I remind you again that black is hard on older or tired people unless they have bright hair and good colouring. Velvet is becoming on most women, especially near the face. Double-purpose coats, rain- or weather-proof, and for day or evening, are a useful development in new fabrics. Most summer dresses require a slip worn underneath and this must usually be of a light colour, or white. When the shade has lost its freshness nylon underwear can be dyed black for winter wear. Some economy-minded women prefer to have lined suits and dresses and do without the necessity to launder slips. In stockings buy the same style and only one or two different shades so that you do not get a lot of odd ones; but should this occur there are excellent dyes.

CARE OF CLOTHES

It is surprising how many women are careless in looking after clothes and footwear. The more hard up you are the more generally well.groomed you should try to be. This does not mean huge bills at the cleaners. First of all buy washable clothes as far as possible. Non-washable coats and suits should be dry brushed on your ironing board and then lightly wet brushed with a bowl of warm water containing a good tablespoon of ammonia. Extra care is usually necessary at the collar and cuffs. Wipe off any excess moisture and put on a hanger to dry. Any difficult stains can be treated with carbon tetrachloride or a similar cleaner which can be bought from a chemist, but always test first where it will not show in case the cleaning fluid is unsuitable for a particular material. Damp press and leave the garments to air. This method will keep most coats, suits, etc., in good order, and the lining should remain clean if other clothes worn are clean too. Gloves should be stretched in position and left flat after use, and shoes need to be brushed, covered with polish and left on trees overnight, and then shined up before use. Stuff very wet shoes with newspaper and allow them to dry before polishing. Shoes should never be placed near direct heat.

Nylon underwear and shirts, which are a real economy in time as they do not require ironing, should be washed out daily and nylon sheets at least weekly. These and many other articles at economy prices can be bought from Brentford Nylons Ltd, who also have a sale-or-return arrangement. *Which?* recommends the local launderette as giving the most economical family wash, and this includes the useful tumble-dry afterwards. If you do not have one within reach a washing machine with spin drier is virtually a 'must' for any mother who does all her washing at home. If you have no washing machine and have in the past sent all the house-

57

hold linen to the laundry it will in the long run be an economy to buy a machine. *Which?* tests domestic equipment and suggests best buys. Reconditioned machines with a six months' guarantee are often available from local electricity board showrooms. Give plenty of thought to the type and size of model you need; if you have an ample domestic hot water supply it will be an extravagance to buy a machine which heats the water and is therefore more expensive to run. If a washing machine is really beyond your means, a spin drier might enable you to cope with the wash.

CARE OF YOUR APPEARANCE

Whatever clothes you choose, remember that thoughtful care of your face and hair will pay dividends. A dull and colourless face should have attention before you start on your outfit. If you choose well and know your most becoming cosmetics these will probably last you quite a long time, especially if they are the kind that can be bought in larger quantities. Buying at a reputable store such as Boots can be an economy. Hairdressing can be an extremely heavy item for any woman and the cost of it is often prohibitive for many widows. It might be worth while looking into the question of buying a wig, as these can be very smart and will serve for special occasions. Some local hairdressers, or further education institutes running hairdressing courses, have a cheap model service. Under this arrangement you can get excellent care of your hair by students under the supervision of experienced people. If you are job-hunting and decide to tint your hair the Hairdressing Council have a list of local reliable hairdressers. Many hairdressers also offer reduced rates at their slack time—for example, Monday 'perms'.

In budgeting for your personal needs you must of course include monthly toilet articles, deodorants, talcum powder, toothpaste, soap, toilet paper, etc. These can mount up very considerably if there are several girls in the family, but again you can save by buying quantity at discount.

Regular dental checks must be included, and here those who are receiving Social Security assistance, or are on a very small income, should get a claim form (F1D), or a receipt from the dentist which can be presented at the Social Security office for payment. This arrangement also covers dentures, spectacles (form F1) and doctor's prescriptions for medicines (form PC11).

It must be remembered that the widowed mother's allowance for herself and her children is unfortunately still very small. In budgeting for clothing for the children, mothers would do well to join or start a clothing exchange at their school so that the children's growth does not lead to too heavy an expense. A uniform and clothing allowance may be available at the school through the education authority. For this the Head should be approached. Teenage daughters should be encouraged to make their own clothes. The children may also have free dinners at school and where necessary you may receive help with travelling expenses.

A mail order firm which prides itself on selling schoolwear 'at the lowest possible price for the quality' is the School Shop, Shambles Street, Barnsley, Yorkshire. It has an extensive catalogue.

Pocket money is a vexed question, but one which must be met up to the time when the child can do a Saturday job or paper round. There will also be Christmas and birthday presents to budget for and minimal entertainment. Inexpensive presents for children to give can be prepared for Christmas by planting indoor bulbs in pots and then tying them up with gay ribbons for the occasion. Some too have an unusual success in raising small pot plants from seeds of fruits, such as an orange or apple pip, or taking geranium cuttings.

'SECONDARY' PRIORITIES

What I call 'secondary' priorities will vary according to numbers and ages of family members. If a widow is by herself a good deal, a television set may well be considered a priority, and if she does not own one already, or has to replace it, one may be hired at a weekly figure of 60p (£1.80 for colour) or be bought on hire purchase. If the latter, the instrument is not hers until all payments are completed, but she does get servicing free during this time. It is wise if you own your own set to insure against major breakdown and repairs, which can run up to £20 or so. The cost of the licence can be difficult to meet, but the Post Office now have a savings card which can be added to each week when allowances are collected. Other equipment, such as radios, record players and bicycles, may all give rise to expenditure in repair and maintenance. Most electrical equipment can be serviced regularly, but this can be costly, and you may prefer to take the risk and forgo this. When replacing is essential, 'trading-in' never offers much, but might provide the down payment for hire purchase of a new model. All such items should be mentioned in the comprehensive insurance cover in case of theft or loss.

The telephone is another item to be budgeted for and is a convenience greatly missed by those used to having one. If possible look at the previous years' bills and estimate what it will cost you; but remember that even if you make fewer and briefer calls, the rental remains the same.

The family may also have pets who should be included in the weekly budget. If the children are given a young animal, such as a cat or dog, it would be wise to accustom either to a mixed diet from the start, so that the expense of pet foods does not become prohibitive. Fresh fish or meat scraps mixed with vegetables cost half of what you may spend on prepared foods and are good for your animals. You do, however, need a refrigerator. The R.S.P.C.A. have details of funds to help with animal illness or operations.

Some mothers regard ballet classes as a priority for their girls. Other children have music or riding lessons. Much depends on the activities followed in your particular environment. Family habits may include smoking and regular film outings. Only when essentials have been covered will you be able to see how much you can spare for what may now appear as luxuries.

In many widows' families routine replacement of curtains, furniture covering, carpets and rugs has to go by the board until the children are out and earning. Some manage to make essential replacements of this kind by discount buying, which allows 10 or 20 per cent off the retail price, but if the family breadwinner has her priorities straight she will put her health and morale first rather than wear herself out trying to maintain standards which other families with a father may keep up. Looking after herself is probably one of the best contributions to the family budget a mother can make.

If, as a widowed mother, you take a job, you will also have to budget your time. Begin by admitting that there is never enough of it and cut out what is not essential in your old routine. Keep a daily jobs list and mark items off as you deal with them. See that as many articles as possible can be machine washed and are non-iron. Plan your meals by the week and cook ahead where possible. Have a weekly and a monthly shopping list and use bulk buying, so that your store cupboard will not let you down. Set breakfast and put out the children's and your own clothes before going to bed, so that you can cut out the early morning rush which can leave you so exhausted. Buy one extra set of basic clothing for each of you, i.e. pants, vests, socks, stockings, etc., and you can avoid last-minute emergencies when articles are not dry. Make your rooms as easy to clean as possible and give storage cupboards priority over other furniture. Make 'don't put it down, put it away' the family motto.

Depending on family attitudes, some widows may wish to insure for private medical care in order to have their choice of specialist or surgeon in serious family sickness. This can be done through the British United Provident Association or the Hospital Service Plan. Many widows have blessed the day when they decided on this special insurance with its varied scales. After all, a period spent in hospital can in this way be much more comfortable and thereby greatly lighten the family's anxiety.

Belonging to such an organization as Cruse is also a worthwhile investment, offering as it does much practical information and help for widows and their children. Members contribute only £1 annually, and for this they can work out their problems with counsellors and in some areas join groups of others dealing with the same practical problems.

INVESTMENTS

If you have the good fortune to inherit a small sum which encourages you to invest, the point needs to be made that, while everyone is looking for absolutely safe, extremely profitable and easily and quickly cashed investments, no such thing exists! People to consult are your bank manager and trustee department, the Corporation of Insurance Brokers, who include life assurance specialists and pension consultants, or one of the qualified financial advisers of a national newspaper or a firm of accountants. The Trustee Savings Bank offers an advisory service to its members on the long-term investment of capital in commerce and industry, and also through Unit Trusts. They operate ordinary savings accounts with a low interest rate, and investment accounts with a much higher interest rate. Invested money may require a month's notice for withdrawal. As the funds are lent to the government the investment is secure. You should note that dividends from building societies are taxed at source, whereas dividends from investments in local authorities are not, and consequently the interest paid by the latter appears larger. For widows whose total income does not require them to pay tax at the standard rate there is no advantage in building society investment, however secure, since this tax deduction cannot be reclaimed. When making an investment of this kind make sure that you understand the terms of withdrawal. The Post Office publish a booklet about their different savings schemes which should also be studied.

If income tax is deducted at source from dividends other than building society, and your income is too low to be taxable, a voucher should be sent to the Inspector of Taxes to claim a refund. This may apply to many older widows. Any appeal against tax assessment must be made to the income tax commissioners. Cruse has a useful Fact Sheet on income tax, and the *Daily Mail* Income Tax Guide (7p) is also worth having.

THE FAMILY CAR

An important asset which you and your husband enjoyed may be your car. If you drive yourself you will hate giving up this considerable convenience, but since even a small car costs to put on the road—including all insurance, taxes, ordinary maintenance and a small allowance for depreciation—approximately £9 per week excluding petrol and VAT charges, this may be a luxury you cannot now afford. In many areas an empty garage can be a luxury too, and produce a weekly income if let.

Do not take a decision to sell your car until you are sure that your financial position will not allow you to keep it. In some circumstances, where there is a big family and you are a distance from school and shopping centre, the car may be a necessity because public transport throughout the year can be difficult, expensive and time consuming for a mother alone. Reduce the car insurance annually to allow for depreciation: its 'up to the minute' value is all you will get if you have to make a claim. From the day it is bought a car loses steadily in value and continues to do so even if you do not put it on the road.

If you do decide to sell your car, seek good advice so that you are not exploited. You can, for example, ask the local A.A. or R.A.C. official, if your husband was a member, to inspect your car and tell you its appropriate price, and these organizations might even provide contact with a buyer. Garages too will usually let you know the approximate second-hand value of your car if you give its year of purchase new. For any transaction you will need the log book, which must not leave your hands until you have cleared the cheque or received cash payment for the car. A potential buyer should never be allowed to make a 'trial run', unless accompanied by you or someone acting on your behalf. The Women Drivers' Association can be a useful contact for you at this time, and it may be helpful to join this organization if you are continuing as a motorist. If possible keep up your driving licence to prevent your having to take the test again should you be able to afford to run a car at a later date. Should payment for a car sale be made by cheque you must never part with the car until your bank has cleared the cheque.

Where other equipment, machinery or now non-usable assets are concerned, you should get advice on selling from knowledgeable people. Again it is unwise to act precipitately or you may get a bad bargain and someone a good one at your expense. Articles which you think may have a value as antiques should be taken to a reputable antique dealer.

If you are arranging any sale of goods most can be advertised in *Exchange & Mart* or in your local paper, using a box number so that you are protected. You may wish to have a business-like friend with you for sale discussions. Know the proper price yourself of any articles, even if you put your advertisement in under 'Any Offers'. Women can have special problems in selling to a man, so if you do not want to commit yourself, or are embarrassed over a suggested sale, you can always say you have someone else coming too, and dismiss your customer by letter or phone later. It is a wise precaution to avoid selling any articles over your doorstep to casual callers.

It goes without saying that if you and your husband were committed to any expenditure such as a holiday arrangement, you should see that this is cancelled, so that the matter is closed.

7

The roof over your head

Your immediate housing position—Considering
the possibilities—House maintenance—Interior
decorating—Neighbourly relations—A source
of income—Conversions—Your garden—
—Moving—Mortgages—Loans—Grants
—Corporate housing schemes.

The comfort of secure housing is a vital necessity when you must go on alone. However difficult all the other problems, to know that the roof over your head is there just as long as you need it is most important for you and your family. Very probably your house is full of happy associations, and is part of your married life. For the children especially it will still be the retreat from the world outside and all its challenge. If, on the other hand, you are now completely alone, you may have extremely mixed feelings, wondering whether you can bear the emptiness. But even if you are in this position, and time spent away with relatives does not help, you are faced with decisions which a widowed mother must make too.

What matters immediately is to know how you stand as an owner, a mortgagee, a leaseholder or a tenant. The house may already be your property, if the mortgage was fully paid, or was covered by life insurance. On the other hand if the mortgage was not secured by an insurance policy you must continue to meet the repayments, with the possibility that the building society will give an extended period for repayment by lower instalments. If you are in rented property a reduction in rent is unlikely unless the house or flat belongs to the local council; the response to such a request may vary in different areas.

Or again, if your husband had just signed a lease for a bigger and more costly house you may find yourself forced to cancel or resell the lease with a nasty financial loss. Should you and your husband have made semi-retirement plans and have been on the verge of a move to a smaller house, but with the signing of all the documents left uncompleted at the time of his death, a quick decision may enable you to change to a flat and carry out your moving plans. If, however, you had no such plans and are deeply attached to your home, to leave it at this time might seem like a further bereavement. Only when you have found your feet and know your weekly income and basic outgoings can you decide whether or not you can afford to live where you are. Clearly then the decision will depend on many things. You may like to list them:

1. All my friends, activities and interests are in this town and area.
2. I could not bear to leave my house and would rather make new plans to cover its maintenance if I possibly can.
3. My children do not want to leave and they should not change schools now.
4. My house could easily be adapted to make flats/flatlets or bed-sitting rooms. I might get a grant for alterations.
5. I am lucky to have a council house and might get rent reduction. On the other hand I may not be allowed to take a lodger, even if I can give up a room. I may be able to exchange my council house for a smaller one in the same area which I like.
6. The rent my husband paid is quite beyond my income as a widow. I must move while I still have enough capital.
7. We had only been here a little while. I have no roots here and want to go to my old home town where I knew everyone. My children's education has barely begun so it would not be disturbed.
8. I cannot bear all the associations with my husband's death here. I must move and get away.
9. I have to earn. There are no jobs here. I am too far from the town and cannot afford the car.
10. Even if I could manage the house I can't see how to cope with the beautiful/large garden. I shan't have time or energy.

Any of these points may be relevant to your situation. I shall consider first the family who want to stay on. If the house or the lease is now yours, put together the last two or more years' maintenance bills and, taking an average, see what you can expect to have to meet in yearly expense: you may already know this if your husband has shared all these matters with you. If the house is in good repair and decoration is fairly recent, you are fortunate. Party walls, fences, and upkeep of the garden, sheds, greenhouse, etc., are all a charge on the future budget. You will have rates to meet too, with or without a rebate.

HOUSE MAINTENANCE

Taking over the management of your house and its repairs on your own is no light matter, and you may find difficulty in getting good and responsible men to do the repairs. You should always get estimates from several reputable firms if possible, and compare them carefully. Keep all your bills for maintenance, including materials such as paint and wallpaper, together with copies of correspondence. Remember also that certain repairs necessitated by, for example, a burst water pipe, may be covered by your insurance policy. Should you be unfortunate with the builder you choose and have a disagreement with him over his work or his bill, for a fee you can get an expert to arbitrate through the Royal Institution of Chartered Surveyors. The National Federation of Building Trades Employers investigate complaints about any work undertaken by their members. If you really cannot find a good painter—sometimes local wallpaper shops or ironmongers know of them—write to the National Federation of Master Painters, who will also investigate complaints about unsatisfactory work carried out by their members.

If you do not own your house your lease may oblige you to repaint the outside in a given time, maybe five or seven years, or to carry out other decorations, and this could well come early in your widowhood if you are unlucky. If you have considerable roof repairs that are urgent you might be able to get a local authority loan to cover the cost. A slated roof is considerably more expensive than a tiled one but lasts a long time. Nowadays rustproof aluminium nails are used for securing slates and make a sound job. Tiles break easily and have a much shorter life. Remember that a builder charges for the erection of scaffolding and even for putting up a roof ladder.

Should you be advised that your house needs electrical rewiring consult the local electricity board as you may get the job done through them on deferred terms if necessary. The National Inspection Council for Electrical Installation Contracting have a list of electricians and will inspect their work for you. (Incidentally, if you have reason to suspect that a maintenance electrician has charged you for repair work he has not done, see your local Weights and Measures Inspector about it.) If you are a tenant of a council or of a private landlord on a lease made after 24th October 1961, according to the 1961 Act it is their responsibility to keep the wiring, gas and water pipes in good order.

Some local authorities give grants for heating installations —especially in newly created smokeless zones. Many house owners have lowered heating costs by fitting insulating material in lofts and attics and by installing double glazing; the latter, however, is expensive.

Turning to plumbing, remember that the Water Board will deal with emergency leaks and fix washers for your taps free. Unofficially they may know a reliable plumber, failing this the Institute of Plumbing will give you the name of a man near you; you can then place any complaints with the institute should they arise. It is wise to have the gutters cleared every autumn and any tiles or slates which have slipped on the roof should be dealt with too. Soakaway drains can be cleared at the same time as they collect leaves and other material during the summer months and should be left clear for the winter rains.

The Ministry of the Environment publishes over sixty advisory leaflets called 'Guides to Good Building' which can be bought from H.M. Stationery Office in London and other main cities or from booksellers. Some of the subjects are of vital concern to home owners: condensation, newer types of paint and their uses, smoky chimneys, watertight basements, dampness in buildings, warmth without waste, painting woodwork, dry rot, frost precautions in household water supply, are only a few. They have a list for you to study.

There is a surprising number of associations to safeguard the consumer. Complaints about approved appliances found to be electrically unsafe will be investigated by the British Electrotechnical Approval Board for Household Equipment; the Electrical Contractors' Association will look into complaints against members. The National House-Builders' Registration Council, Federation of British Carpet Manufacturers, British Horological

Institute (clocks and watches), Radio and TV Retailers' Association, Association of British Launderers and Cleaners and the Patients' Association will all investigate complaints. The National Federation of Consumer Groups, 14 Buckingham Street, London WC2N 6DS can tell you of others.

INTERIOR DECORATING

'Do it Yourself' is an obvious economy here, but if you are unpractised at it, or do not like climbing ladders, you can compromise by having ceilings done professionally and tackling walls and paintwork yourself. In some parts of the country it is not easy to find a decorator to take on small jobs, so remember that one is more likely to be available in the winter months when bad weather prevents outside work. In circumstances of hardship certain men's organizations will sometimes give voluntary help in decorating jobs. Where young people volunteer to help they must be known to be responsible, and supervision of the more skilled jobs is advisable or materials may be wasted and the job have to be redone. When buying materials for use in the maintenance of your house, discount buying of well-known products can be a saving. Thornfield Ltd sell top quality branded paints, lino tiles, 'Vinolay', 'Cosywrap' for lofts or tanks and many other materials at good percentage reductions. Carriage is paid only on some goods. Write for details, colour charts, etc.

It is surprising how often new and remarkable materials and do-it-yourself aids come on to the market. A visit to a building centre will offer you a great deal of information and free literature; there are building centres in London, Bristol, Manchester and other towns. A look round your local decorating shops can also be extremely fruitful, and you will nowadays usually find an understanding and well-informed salesman to advise you. Polystyrene in many forms, principally tiles, for bad ceilings, behind baths, and for walls, can be very cheap and practical. Adhesive lino tiles are easier for a woman to fix than a roll of lino. They wear well and can be replaced singly. They, or heavy-quality Fablon, are admirable for shelves. Know your paint shops too, as variety of colour in paints on walls, woodwork or floors can make a transformation in any room. One wall repainted in a fresh colour can work wonders and costs very little. Painted walls, of course, do require a good surface; where it is poor, papering may be best and dextrine can be mixed with cold-water paste to make the thicker papers adhere well. Special paper is sold for kitchens and bathrooms. One useful tip while on a painting job is to keep your paint brushes in aluminium foil overnight and save having to clean them. Reader's Digest publish *The Good Handyman's Encyclopaedia*, which may prove very useful; and there is *Handyman Which?*—back numbers can be obtained for 60p each. Many local institutes of further education run classes in decorating and woodwork. It is very certain that if you have decided to make your house 'work for its living', you must inform yourself fully on all that this involves in practical care and economy. Finally, be sure that your own comprehensive house insurance covers accidents to anyone working on your premises.

NEIGHBOURLY RELATIONS

One source of friction in neighbourly relations can be the care of party walls and fences, and also overhanging and tall trees and climbing shrubs which become a nuisance to those living next door. It is helpful to know exactly for what you are responsible and to have a clear understanding with your neighbour about this. Each owner has a right to have a party wall or fence maintained and has liability for its maintenance and repair. With regard to overhanging trees, where the branches of a tree belonging to an owner overhang the soil of an adjoining landowner or occupier, the latter may at any time cut off any branch which overhangs his land without notice to the former. He must not trespass on the adjoining land to do this. On the other hand, the branches which are cut off, and any fruit on them, belong to the owner of the tree. There is no decided legal case on the matter of trees obstructing light, but if a creeper grows on to an adjoining house and blocks the gutter it is the responsibility of the owner of the creeper to take the necessary action.

Should quarrels regarding these matters develop between neighbours a state of exasperation and annoyance can be reached where life becomes very miserable indeed. A widow can ill afford to have unhappy relations of this kind. Once legal help is openly sought, relationships tend to deteriorate and it is probably better to discuss such problems with the Citizens' Advice Bureau or to have a private talk with a solicitor on the Legal Aid list. Cruse has a Fact Sheet on obtaining Legal Aid. The AA *Family Guide to the*

Law is a useful reference book which could be consulted at the library.

YOUR HOUSE A SOURCE OF INCOME

Your house, probably your largest asset, may have to make money for you. This can be done, for example, by 'doubling up' children of the same sex in one room with, if necessary, bunk beds, thus leaving a room free as a bed-sitter for letting or for a paying guest to live with the family. Two rooms freed can be an even more profitable proposition. Where there are exceptionally large rooms in a big house and a number of children to accommodate, wardrobes and cupboards can be placed down the centre of the room to form a practical division. Creating a children's room can ease any friction between young members of the family and paying guests.

Some widows, especially those living alone, are encouraged to take students as boarders to eke out their incomes. This can work well if the widow likes young people. Most universities allow only £5·50 for a five-day week, with breakfast and supper included, and £7 for seven days, with full board at the weekends. When you consider that this must cover food for a hungry youngster, heating, lighting, baths and washing of laundry, plus the considerable wear and tear of your home, you will see there is little room for profit. Such a sum too barely covers the extra work, cooking or shopping involved. On the other hand, you might make a financial success of it if the young people share rooms or cubicle rooms. Freehold ownership allows you to make interior alterations to your home, and if an undertaking is made with the university to take in students on a regular basis, they may be willing to pay for, or contribute towards, the cost of such conversion as would make the whole arrangement financially worth while for you. You will be able to talk over the practical side of the planning with the special university visitor whose job it is to look after students who are in lodgings.

The cost and method of heating are important where separate room arrangements are made, so the installation of some form of easily managed central heating system, if your house lacks it, may be a worth-while capital expenditure. This, however, needs very careful consideration. Some households have found night storage off-peak electric central heating a good investment. So much extravagance can occur over the use of individual gas or electric

70

fires that they can be a liability where there are paying guests or tenants, unless you have separate meters which can usually be hired from the gas or electricity company at a quarterly rent, the setting for gas supply to be fixed by the gas fitter. 'Ascots' or similar types of gas water heaters are excellent as they give any number of baths immediately, and heat the water only when it is wanted.

If you give service such as cooking and cleaning you can treat profits as earned income. From 6th April 1973, Earned Income Relief is abolished with the introduction of a unified system of income tax, but the Tax Commissioner will set certain allowances against income in assessing a widow's tax position; and this will include any repairs or improvements made during the year. If you decorate your boarders' rooms yourself you can claim for materials but not for your labour; if you employ someone to do the job you may claim for the lot.

CONVERSION OF HOUSE TO FLATS

Bathroom and toilet facilities are most important and additions may be needed. It is worth looking into the cost of installing a shower rather than a bath as there can be considerable saving in hot water and less irritation over the use of the shower room if there are many people to use it. Local authority grants can be secured where a separate flat is being made available for letting and an additional bathroom, lavatory, kitchen or larder are needed. A formal application must be made to the housing department and, if approved, the owner may receive a grant of up to half the cost of the work done. It is essential to discuss this with the local authority and with your solicitor or surveyor before approaching a builder, and written approval from the local authority must be in your hands before the work is started. A council grant does not have to be repaid, and there are few strings attached. There are no restrictions on selling the home after it has been improved with the help of a grant. If the house would divide into several independent flats careful weighing up of the considerable cost may show that such letting could give you financial security and the right housing for yourself up to old age. Tax relief is allowed on interest payable on money borrowed for such a purpose, provided that all relevant documents and accounts are kept. But such a step should not be undertaken without full professional advice. There is a Consumers' Association publication

Extending your House (£1) setting out the points to be considered, and there are firms who specialize in conversion or extension work. Elite Loft Conversions, for example, have a pre-constructed scheme costing between £600 and £1,200 which they can complete in five days.

If you are letting a room or a flat, furnished or unfurnished, there are booklets available at Citizens' Advice Bureaux or the Town Hall covering the questions and answers of landlord and tenant, rents and responsibilities. Other ways of using your house if you have nursing qualifications include turning it into a small geriatric unit caring for old people, or running a nursery. In either case permission must be sought from the local authority and an inspection of the premises will be made. Cloakroom and lavatory facilities and fire precautions are important. There is considerable demand for both types of service and an enterprising woman can make a great success of either. The income in all cases must be entered for tax, but an allowance is made for all outgoing expenses, including wear and tear, rent and rates and other incidental costs.

The suggestion that a widow should share her home with another is often made and comes mainly from the lonely owner. This means that another woman must trust her luck and reception with no security at all, and the risk that an unsatisfactory relationship may leave her homeless is always there. Such an arrangement may work better with some form of written agreement. If, however, one of the widows is homeless in special circumstances and has no furniture of her own, she may be glad of a home in exchange for services. References as to character and personality are as important as those relating to honesty and domestic ability if the scheme is to work well. A trial period may well be desirable on both sides.

YOUR GARDEN

If you decide to remain where you are you will need to think of your garden too, and if you have loved your own plot you will hate to see it fall into neglect. To budget for a gardener, even if you can get one, may be impossible. A great deal will depend on your own keenness and ability as a gardener, as well as on the size of garden. Do you, as a working widow, want to cut down the work to a minimum, or, as a widowed mother with growing children, want to make your garden as productive as possible? If so you may want to reconsider layout as soon as you can. A vegetable garden and fruit trees can be very important for those with a family but, if time is more valuable to you than home-grown produce, you may decide to alter the borders, extend the grass area or plant shrubs to cut down work.

Planning afresh will in any case give you an interest and something to look forward to. A rose garden is easy to maintain, as are borders of flowering shrubs and ground-cover plants rather than annuals. Grass cutting can be done on contract, but this can be expensive, although it will not be necessary from about December to April. If you have your own mower you may be able to find someone willing to do the work for a small weekly sum. If your garden is very small, paving stones instead of lawn, and wine barrels bought from wine distributors and cut in half instead of flower borders, can make an easy-to-work garden. The tubs can be planted with roses, dahlias, climbing strawberries or annuals and add character to a small patio. Some local councils have broken paving stone for sale, but if you intend the alteration from garden to patio to be permanent it is worth having the ground properly levelled and prepared. Paths can be surfaced with boiler ash waste, cold asphalt (do-it-yourself) or a load of small shingle from the builder's yard or a quarry.

If you intend seriously to make your garden productive, you will find that belonging to a local gardening club not only offers the opportunity of meeting a quite new group of enthusiasts, but may also enable you to recoup much of the subscription by obtaining at a reduced price garden goods such as fertilizers, seeds, plants, etc., through the organizer. It will also help the woman who is alone, and who from time to time needs advice or male assistance with heavy jobs. Most keen gardeners are very willing to be helpful—and flattered to be asked. You can quickly learn how to prune roses and shrubs, but fruit trees need a practised eye and probably a tall ladder: the gardening club will almost certainly be able to put you in touch with someone to do the job. A garden will not continue to give good crops unless you put something back into the soil. The cheapest form of fertilizer after your own compost heap is without doubt to be found at your nearest sewage farm where you can usually get powdered sewage, which is odourless and pleasant to use, and is sold ready in $\frac{1}{2}$-cwt. bags

at a reasonable price. You will, however, need a car to make
the collection, but it may be possible to arrange this with one or
two other friends or Cruse Club members so that each has a
reasonable quantity. Sulphate of ammonia fertilizer is obtainable from gas boards cheaply.

If you have a greenhouse, you might usefully come to some
arrangement with a neighbour or club member who is without one
whereby he makes use of it to raise plants from seed for both your
gardens; or, if you are a non-gardening working widow, a neighbour might use your greenhouse to raise tomatoes and give you a
share of the crop. The really green-fingered widow might even
consider renting an allotment from the council, but this does call
for hard work and continuous attention if it is to be worth while.
She will, however, be surrounded by other enthusiasts.

To get full advantage from a really productive garden you
should consider buying a deep-freeze unit; second-hand ice-cream
cabinets are often obtainable and cost little to run. Freezing soft
fruits and vegetables such as peas, beans and Brussels sprouts is
quick and easy to do, and the produce retains a good flavour.
Deep Freezing is an A–Z guide on how to stock and maintain a
deep freeze; 10p, or 13p from the publishers, Kenneth Mason,
Homewell, Havant, Hants. However, if you have only a small
surplus for preserving, jam-making and bottling will meet your
needs. Pulped apples are especially useful for pies and sauces and
preserve well.

Finally, there are many books available on all aspects of gardening, and your local library or Garden Centre will certainly
have a good selection.

IF YOU DECIDE TO MOVE

I turn now to those who decide to move. First of all you have the
important decision regarding where you wish to live. If you have
children, schools and easy transport are extremely important; you
also require to be near good shops for economy shopping. If you
are alone you can suit yourself over your social needs, which are
going to be important. It may be possible for you to move nearer
to relatives and old friends. Your thoughts may turn to a seaside
resort, where, however, there will probably be a preponderance of
elderly people in the off season and a great increase of visitors and
considerable discomfort during the high season; on the other

74

hand, if you take a seaside flat or house, seasonal lettings might make it possible for you to travel abroad or to another part of the country in the summer months. If you decide to move to a different town, or into a town from the country or outer suburbs, there will be the possibility of full- or part-time work for you in addition to social amenities. In Cecil Chisholm's book, *Retire and Enjoy It*, there is an appendix listing places which in many ways favour retirement, and giving details about the population, the climate, the nature of the surrounding country, the rainfall and soil for gardeners. Although the figures given for rates, and in some cases for population, are now out of date, it would be well worth while studying this if you are not familiar with many seaside and country towns in Britain. If you have no special connection with a particular town, but have a general interest in it, you can write to the department of employment to ask what the work situation would be for you there, and also to the Citizens' Advice Bureau to find out whether there is a community centre and what social amenities you and your family can expect. It is equally important to know about public transport if you no longer have a car. Should the children be young, and due soon to go to primary or secondary school, you will need to know about schools before moving; the local education authority will help here. Other important factors are your own age and health. If you are inclined to rheumatism or arthritis you should avoid clay soil, damp conditions and cutting winds. Should you not expect to move again, choose the type of housing which is going to meet your situation as you grow older and are less able to tackle housework.

When examining the question of moving, do not forget to allow for removal expenses, the probable need for new curtains and curtain runners, stair-carpet fittings, floor coverings, perhaps extra or different furniture (second-hand furniture does not often fetch very good prices). When looking over houses make a point of noting if there are adequate built-in cupboards, light fittings, wall plugs, kitchen units, and the general state of decoration and any essential repairs needed. It is wise to make a complete list of all likely expenses so as to be sure that you can afford to make the move you propose, and know how much money you must have available.

Selling or buying property is a complicated business to a lay person. If in doubt on any point, your solicitor (whom you pay to watch your interests) is there to advise you. You may also like to consult the Cruse Fact Sheet on 'Buying or Selling a House'.

In selling a house of which you are the owner-occupier you are not liable for capital gains tax on any profit made on the original purchase price. If there is an outstanding mortgage on your house the building society (or other mortgagor) will of course hold the deeds, so that although you may put your house up for sale without consulting the mortgagor the transaction cannot be completed until the mortgage has been paid off from the proceeds of the sale, and the deeds transferred. In practice, especially if it is your intention to buy a smaller house, it is advisable to inform the building society, who will probably be prepared to transfer the mortgage to the new property, if required, provided they are satisfied that in your altered financial position you will be able to keep up the repayments and that the house you want to buy is a worthwhile purchase. If you are able to pay off the mortgage from the proceeds of selling your house and do not intend to buy another, any profit is of course yours.

Transfer of deeds must be done through your solicitor, but you do not have to sell a house through an estate agent if you do not wish to and have sufficient confidence in your business ability to carry the transaction through. Remember that, even if a deposit is paid, the transaction is not final until the contract is signed; if as a buyer you pay a deposit on a house, make sure that the receipt contains the words 'subject to contract'. Most widows, however, would be wiser to put their house in the hands of an estate agent, even though this means paying his commission, for his knowledge of the market and of procedure might well obtain a better price and quicker sale for you. There are reputable firms of estate agents almost everywhere, but if you are in doubt consult your friends or your solicitor. Even if everything goes smoothly, the transaction is not likely to be completed in less than two months, and it might take much longer. If you want to buy a house before your own is sold you may have to seek a bridging loan from the bank on which (if you get one) you will have to pay interest. Speed of sale can therefore be important.

Some widows wish to move from rented property into a house of their own, and therefore seek to obtain a mortgage. Here much will depend on your income and earning capacity. If you or your late husband were in what is called 'public service' the

Civil Service Housing Association may help you with a mortgage through the Civil Service Building Society, which lends on flats and maisonettes. Apparently the National Association of Local Government Officers Building Society has a larger number of women borrowers than most.

The Government Option Mortgage Scheme, which can enable the borrower to borrow the whole of the purchase money on a house, should also be studied. Most people pay less tax as a result of taking out a mortgage. The Option Mortgage Scheme gives the choice of foregoing tax relief in return for a Government subsidy which reduces the interest on the mortgage. The advance required is guaranteed by an insurance policy, with the Government sharing the risk equally with the insurance company. As a result the borrower pays a reduced premium.

Widows can get mortgages if their circumstances are favourable, but it must be recognized that in some cases their position hardly commends itself to a lender, who naturally wants to be satisfied that the borrower's means fit the commitment. But do not allow yourself to be too easily put off. Building societies differ in their conditions, and what is rejected by one may be accepted by another. A building society which knows you because you have already had a mortgage with them may give more favourable consideration; so may any society with whom you have deposited savings. Three building societies to approach are the Co-operative Permanent, the Church of England Building Society and the Abbey National. If your own financial status is marginal, you may still get a mortgage if you are able to find a substantial guarantor.

Remember that some local authorities are comparatively liberal in the way they administer house purchase schemes. Some lenders do not favour older borrowers; others will lend to people up to the age of sixty, provided the advance required is not more than three-quarters of the value of the house, and provided the borrower's income is likely to continue. Most local authorities would expect repayment by the age of sixty-five.

It is possible to obtain a conversion grant under the 1969 Housing Act, and you should apply to your own Local Authority for details. A building society such as the Property Owners lends at a lower rate to an owner occupier than to an owner converting a property for letting. The Chelsea and South London

Building Society gives conversion loans, but borrowers must have been saving with the society for at least a year. The money may be paid in stages but is rarely handed over totally in advance of the completion of the work. A bridging loan can sometimes be secured from the bank on receipt of a letter of acceptance from the society.

Evidence of health is not normally required, unless you wish to include life assurance provision with your mortgage, which is a wise thing to do for your dependants. Life assurance will be required if you borrow from an insurance company, but before choosing this type of mortgage you should weigh up very carefully whether it is appropriate in your circumstances.

If the day comes when you, as a householder, are over sixty-nine, and your budget just won't stretch far enough any longer, you can make use of your house to enlarge your income. Under the Save and Prosper Group Plan it is possible to take out a mortgage which will bring you in an annuity while you continue to enjoy your home. The house remains yours to leave to relatives, and the advanced moneys are paid off out of your total estate. If the house is sold on your death any increase in value belongs to the estate. Widows who are over sixty-five are advised to study the Consumers' Association publication entitled 'Arrangements for Old Age'. There is a useful section on housing and other valuable information.

CORPORATE HOUSING AND HOUSING ASSOCIATIONS

There are various possibilities in corporate non-profit-making housing which could be of interest to widows and it is worth while for you to know the details. Schemes can cover the buying of a new house for yourself and your children in a housing group or joining in an association where old property is being altered. If a group of widows or friends want to start a housing association the people who are in touch with such groups all over the country are the National Federation of Housing Societies. From the Federation you can also obtain the leaflet on government loans to housing associations. Loans for a co-operative housing scheme are available too from the Housing Corporation. For schemes which cover corporate ownership a suitable house must be found in the first place and here the papers with wide cover are *Daltons, Property Advertiser, Homefinder, Houses & Estates*. For the Greater

London area, the *London Property Letter* gives a great deal of up-to-date information and the *Property Hunters' Index* has similar cover. It may be possible to consult these in a reference library.

Detailing the three forms of association, these are:

1. Co-ownership Associations   These have a rule that every member must be a tenant (or potentially one) and every tenant must be a member. The finance is provided (100 per cent) two-thirds by a Building Society and one-third by the Housing Corporation. A co-ownership home combines some of the advantages of renting property with that of owning it. Deposit and legal fees are comparatively small (between £50 and £200), the co-owner can leave at short notice and without expense, and if you stay more than five years you share in any increase in the value of the home. It costs little or nothing to join the waiting list for a co-ownership house. For a complete list of current developments, write to the Housing Corporation's head office (Sloane Square House, London SW1W 8NT). As soon as a house is available, the prospective member joins the housing society by buying a £5 share. Contributions made to the association are in the form of rent, and the Ministry of Social Security is prepared to take this into consideration if the tenant is in receipt of supplementary benefit.

2. Charitable Associations   These normally get 90 per cent or 100 per cent mortgages from their local authorities. They are entitled to subsidies from government funds and may be allowed contributions in addition from the local rates. Rents are calculated to meet mortgage repayments and the cost of administration. This is a very well-established form of housing association and the Federation will provide all details.

3. Housing Aid Societies   These work on the principle of getting the best possible value for money and making the maximum use of the potential of those it tries to help. There are a variety of schemes aimed at young couples just starting out and also for fatherless families. They are half-way houses for those paying excessive rents to enable them to save (possibly incorporating compulsory saving in the rent). Guidance is also given through the complexities of house purchase and with specialist help the applicant can have his or her case put to the committee and, if agreed, implemented.

Considering the possibilities from the widow's point of view it may well be that a scheme intended to accommodate different types of family situations would be the happiest: that is to say some complete families, some students, some elderly people, some unsupported mothers, etc. For many widows loneliness is one of the most difficult of their personal problems, and any housing scheme which will bring the tenants together is obviously going to be the best one. For this reason a house which has a common lounge where members meet regularly, either for committee or in social activities, would be better than one where each family unit is completely isolated. Another valuable factor in a corporate scheme can be the inclusion of a 'mother figure' who has concern for all the people living together and will help to bind them into a happy unit; such a person must of course be chosen with very great care and should never be the bossy type. Women who have had the independence of running their own home retain quite a strong desire for this factor in living, and even in shared property they still need to feel that their part is definitely their own to which they can invite their friends and their family without having to draw in other members of the house group unless they wish. In some housing schemes there is a guest room which can be booked by residents for those they wish to invite to stay with them.

Where house conversions are the aim the local authority may give a Discretionary Grant of half the cost, up to a maximum of £1,000. Where a property of three or more storeys is converted into flats, the maximum is £1,200 for each flat. A Council grant does not have to be repaid. A loan, or second mortgage, would be repayable over twenty-five to thirty years, and would be granted subject to certain conditions. The first person to approach if this type of housing scheme is being considered is the town clerk, as it is the concern of all local government officers to increase housing facilities in the neighbourhood. Interest-free loans and gifts from friends of the scheme are welcome, and Charities may also participate.

There are many housing societies likely to be of interest to widows. I can list only a few of them: The Carr/Gomm Society Ltd; Shelter Housing Aid Centre incorporating the Catholic

Housing Aid Society; Mutual Households Association; the Housing Association for Officers' Families; the British Churches Housing Trust; Widow's Friend Society; the Miss Edith Urch Housing Schemes; Harding Housing Association; Abbeyfield Societies; the Civil Service Housing Association; Enfield Housing Association; Douglas Haig Memorial Homes; Samaritan Housing Association; United Women's Homes Association; W.R.V.S. Housing Schemes; the Samuel Lewis Dwellings Trust and the Sutton Dwellings Trust.

The Housing Centre Trust is also a useful organization to know about, as it acts as a clearing house for information on every aspect of housing within its organization.

COST-RENT AND CO-OWNERSHIP SCHEMES

If you are looking for a modern home in a cost-rent or co-ownership scheme the Housing Corporation publish a directory giving addresses of housing of this kind all over the country. They also state the type of housing, i.e. houses, flats or maisonettes, and whether plans are in preparation and the building not yet started, or the scheme is under construction or complete and ready to receive applications for vacancies. The booklet also contains an alphabetically arranged list of societies.

THE GUARDIAN HOUSING ASSOCIATION

The Guardian Housing Association (97 St Aldates, Oxford) has recently been launched to provide one- or two-bedroomed flats for over-sixties who have a little capital, possibly through selling their own, too-large, homes. Occupiers are asked to loan about £8,000; this sum is returnable if you leave, or it can be willed to relatives less a small percentage. There is security for life, with the benefit of central heating and background care facilities. The Association is interested in hearing of building plots of half to one and a half acres, for which they could negotiate, or possibly of large houses suitable for conversion. Schemes are already under way in seven different parts of the country. Over-sixties without capital may discuss their needs with the Help the Aged Housing Association at the same address.

The important thing to remember in regard to all housing plans is that if it is at all possible these should not be hurried, and this is especially true in regard to forming a housing association. It can

81

take quite a long while to work through the detailed procedure, and in the first place it is important that those who are interested should write in for details and then study the whole matter together with someone with some experience of this kind of approach. It may well be that through such an organization as Cruse, a local club with its supporting committee may wish to go into this matter on behalf of its own members who are dissatisfied with their housing. Many widows live in properties far too big for them, often encountering great loneliness and even fear. Obviously it is in the interest of the country's housing shortage that full advantage should be taken of existing provisions for bringing women together when they wish this, in satisfactory schemes which will allow them independence and a financial commitment within their means.

8

Work in widowhood

A realistic attitude to the working world—Need for imaginative official approach to a widow's problems—Research study of working women —The jobs many do—On not working to capacity—Raising a family not a life's work —The educated and the trained woman —Capitalizing skills—Work with people—In schools—For children and young people—For the sick and disabled—No training required—'Outwork'—Some bright ideas —Having paying guests—Mail-order agent —Starting a business.

This chapter is going to be both a challenge and a spur. I hope that it will be helpful and realistic and give you many practical ideas about work and earning. To suggest that widows find it easy to return to work from marriage without a previous professional training might give you courage, but it would hardly represent the truth. For the majority this is a difficult but necessary step to take; necessary because money is short and the pension inadequate, hard because our working world is still largely reluctant to go out of its way to take the married woman back, although there are many callings where she might help to fill a gap. Thoroughly accustomed to the independence of the home, doing what she likes more or less when she likes, it can be understood that the woman returning to work after widowhood can feel ill at ease in the world of industry, commerce and the professions with their strict hours and essential disciplines. The need is to find an effective bridge.

For the widow, sudden tragedy forces rapid adaptation to new circumstances and often leaves little time for her to consider training or re-training. There is no more regular money from the husband and too few men leave capital to cushion their wives over the transition from exclusive home cares to those of the outside working world. This, too, would be the best time for many women to receive a capital sum from pension sources, if only this were part of the national statutory plan. Those with dependants in the home and transport problems are tempted to take the nearest job, which may pay poorly and be of low status. The 'little job' and 'light job' are often what a widow looks for or what she gets, but usually they by no means represent her real capacity. Encouragement to discuss her abilities and potential is as important as the provision of suitable training and grant aid to put her on to her feet. In numerical strength alone, widows in this country could provide a great contribution to national productivity. Furthermore, re-employment in a satisfying job can give widows a renewed sense of purpose. Hoped-for changes for the better in the woman's working world include a fairer adjustment reached through equal pay for equal work. Other changes are needed too: in income tax rulings which now class a widow as a single person while she still retains the same responsibility as in marriage; in income-related grant aid for teacher training; in imaginative statutory care and thought for her fatherless children, including substantial tax allowance for domestic help; in sick pay and holiday pay pro rata for part-time work, and the relaxation of rigid age concepts which can waste several decades of productive years after a woman reaches forty.

In a working future you as a widow need not only strength of purpose but a new view of your own possibilities. If you have, in the past, taken the 'protected' part in marriage, widowhood may launch you into new discoveries about yourself as a person with a part to play beyond the four walls of your home. It is even possible that, after the sheltered years you have had in marriage, you will enjoy the stimulus of difficulty and achievement which is wholly your own. In a research study of working women in their middle years Le Gros Clark found that one in nine of the working women studied between the ages of forty-five and sixty-nine were widows, and of these forty-three per cent were in personal service as cooks, kitchen hands and domestic helps. Dressmakers, bookbinders, typists and clerks return to their skills in widowhood, and the managerial capacities of married women seemed after widowhood to attract them to proprietorship of confectionery or newspaper shops, where their numbers were relatively high. Other jobs where domestic skills were apparently made use of were food processing and the laundry industry. Younger widows frequently worked as shop assistants, but opportunities here tended to diminish with age.

As a whole, women are practical in their view of things and are quick to see that middle age can be a danger point when there has been no earlier training. It is interesting to note that the percentage of women entering higher education in 1971 was only 12·2; 4·8 per cent of women entered university in the same year. Not so long ago there was a commonly held belief that women had less intellectual capacity than men. Now it is accepted that men and women have equal intelligence and both need training in a great variety of skills at the right time. Nevertheless many older women did not grow up with a working life in view. Nearly 60 per cent of full-time adult women workers today earn less than £20 a week. The official weekly earnings in Great Britain (1973) show that the average for women is half that of men. Non-manual male workers average £43·4 weekly, women £22·1; male manual workers (industry and services) average £35·82 weekly, women £18·30. It is interesting to set these figures against the statutory £20 weekly family subsistence level below which supplementary benefit is payable. However, in 1975 the equal pay for equal work legislation is due to take effect in all areas of work where this does not exist already.

We are below strength in many professions which are well-suited to women: solicitors, veterinary surgeons and teachers, dieticians, medical social workers, librarians, occupational therapists, radiographers. In the child care services there is a great need for more day nurseries and registered child minders, while the shortage of nursing personnel is also common knowledge. I recognize that nursing is a calling requiring considerable dedication, a fairly arduous training and love of hospital life, or, one could add, of sick people. Many widows have had tragic experiences which they associate with hospitals, and are not thereafter much drawn to them even though they now have a special knowledge of what death itself means. Increasingly the role of home help, in the very kindly and special service it offers to people in difficulty, is one which widows can fill. Nevertheless an up-grading of pay will be required here.

It is my purpose in this book to deal with situations as they are, so the undoubted difficulties encountered by the working widow or the widow seeking work must be emphasized. Women themselves will be the first to recognize that they must set to work to prepare themselves for a more exacting and rewarding role in life. They have much to give to the community, and without their abilities and skills the burdens are unfairly distributed. To raise children is no longer a lifetime's work.

If you as a widow have a personal background of higher education or professional training you are fortunate. Even if you are hesitant about returning to your calling the capacity to organize your life and family will support you in such difficulties as you may meet. If you are out of touch with your profession you will need an up-to-date picture of how things are now, and this can be obtained through the British Federation of University Women, and through the Women's Employment Federation, whose excellent book *Careers for Girls and Women* is now in its twenty-third edition (60p including postage). Cruse Fact Sheet on Training and Work Opportunities for the Older Woman should be consulted. It contains much useful information relevant to the social problems a woman in this position is likely to encounter and gives practical suggestions, including addresses and other details she may need. The Gentlewomen's Work and Help Society offers training grants and finds markets for handwork and needlework. Fine needlework can also be sold through the Women's Home Industries; *Woman's Own* have a list of well-known firms who employ outside knitters. A first step might be to join the local branch of the National Housewives' Register, which is a meeting point for shared interests. HER (Home Enterprises Register) is another scheme, started by the National Association of Women's Clubs to help housebound women who want to earn.

Such jobs as beauty therapy, demonstrating, corsetry, and domestic arts, needlework, knitting, sewing, cooking, horticulture and floristry are perhaps less demanding than work requiring long training. The Priscilla Lobley flower kits might start one off on a money-making hobby. The kits are priced from 75p. Dressmaking can be undertaken at home or as an employee for finishing, altering or mending garments for shops, manufacturers or dry cleaners. Cooking possibilities include the school meals service, institution management, general and freelance catering. Part-time cooking jobs can often be found.

Market research is a job that is now well established, and many widowed mothers value its flexible working hours. It requires some education and the ability to conduct interviews. Training courses are arranged and preferences noted as to the areas where work can most conveniently be done. Those interested in analysis coding for punch-card operating or in research may find a readier welcome if they are over thirty-five. A Market Research list can be obtained from Cruse.

In offices there are increasing demands for staff, for both the newly trained and those women with secretarial qualifications who have taken refresher courses if long absent from work. Applicants should be prepared to take tests at interviews and to have good speeds. To gain experience it is worth while to take voluntary or temporary jobs and then ask for a written reference. Office jobs cover receptionists, clerical workers, telephonists and office machine operators. Work to be done at home, so often sought by widowed mothers with young children, is not easy to come by unless tape, audio or dictaphone typing has been learned or the widow has a duplicating machine of her own. Older women can be in demand as medical secretaries, but they are advised to make themselves proficient in medical technical terms before applying for work in this sphere. A dictionary of medical terms is a great help. Part-time jobs are often offered and sometimes evening hours. School secretaryships are much in demand, both by widowed mothers with school-age children who wish to share their holidays, and by older widows who have the time to enjoy the human interest of the work. Those who have clerical qualifications only should approach the Department of Employment, local secretarial agencies, secretarial colleges who run agency facilities for clients and for their students; or advertise in local newspapers, or apply direct to local authority offices. Women up to forty without previous experience, or up to fifty-nine if they have previous experience, are needed as G.P.O. telephonists. Training is with pay and, of course, the job itself carries the advantages of the Civil Service.

There are openings for women in all types of museums: national, local authority, educational, university, hospital and private. A wide range of cultural knowledge is covered and technical assistants prepare and repair museum exhibits. There are also openings for cataloguers and guide lecturers. For national museums the Civil Service Commission should be approached. Some women are practised speakers and now may have time to undertake lecturing, voluntarily on the panel of, for example, the Women's Institute or Townswomen's Guild, or professionally through a lecture agency, such as Foyles of London, the Workers' Educational Association, or the National Institute of Adult Education. Of course, qualifications must be given, and it would be wise to include a draft half-hour talk when applying. Fees and expenses will be paid for professional work.

The government's Training Opportunities Scheme (TOPS) provides a chance of learning a new skill or improving an old one. It offers free courses in a wide range of subjects up to management level, and including commercial and clerical work. The facilities are available at colleges of further education, government training centres and on employers' premises. Tax-free allowances ranging from £8·75 to £19 a week are paid during instruction, and at the end of the course the Department of Employment's placement services help trainees to find employment suited to their new skills. Courses can last from one month (for brushing up secretarial skills for example, before returning to work) to one year. They are usually full-time, but some operate on a more flexible basis. Details about TOPS and the courses it offers are given at any local employment office of the Department of Employment.

For other professional work, with the possibility either of training or of refresher courses, there are a number of advisory services, in addition to the Department of Employment, which it is useful to know. These include the Women's Employment Federation, the Nursing Recruitment Service, and the Over Forty Association for Women Workers. The last is a voluntary body which offers an advisory service for older women who have problems of employment and housing.

Graduates, either with or without teaching diplomas, and those holding teacher training certificates, will know of the need for either part- or full-time teachers. The Department of Education and Science strongly recommends that widows who are seeking grants to start a teacher-training course should have a personal interview with a senior official at the L.E.A., as special arrangements are made for assessing awards for widows. Most local education authorities have arrangements for short refresher courses, and some have grant-aided courses for women over sixty who are still active and alert. It may be difficult or even impossible to take a training/refresher course if you are over fifty, but any woman who has had useful experience in the past should find a way of using this. Those who lack the minimum entry qualifications for teacher training college should direct their inquiries to the local education office regarding grants. The house-bound can study at home for a degree with or without L.E.A. help. Write to the National Extension College, Cambridge. *The Times Educational Supplement, The Teacher* and *Teacher's World* are useful papers to consult. The Workers' Educational Association may have work in evening class teaching. Those suitably qualified can find work coaching privately or marking exam papers. The Educational Grants Advisory Service exists to help all students with doubts and difficulties to be resolved, and can be reached through the National Council of Social Service, 26 Bedford Square, London WC1.

The National Council of Social Service arranges both training and refresher courses for work in different fields of social service. There are many women who have a natural compassion for ageing people, and certainly there are few groups that need their help more. Work possibilities include administrative posts as welfare secretaries, organizers for sheltered workshops, and managerial posts in old people's homes. Short training courses with grant aid are available for selected candidates. The National Corporation for the Care of Old People is a key organization to know.

The Young Women's Christian Association offers scope for initiative, a chance to experiment and an opportunity for international contacts to those trained in social work, youth work, teaching or domestic science. Write to the personnel department.

The diploma in Social Administration can be taken internally at the London School of Economics; this is a two-year course for people over twenty, with no upper age limit. The normal university entrance qualifications are not required, but the London School of Economics set their own general entrance paper. Hillcroft College, Surbiton, Surrey, has both a one- and a two-year course. Application can be made to local education authorities for grants to cover both courses. The same studies may be done through university extension lectures (day time and evening) at main institutes of further education or through London University. Inquiries should be directed to the local institute.

There are special courses in the Probation Service for candidates over thirty. The secretary of the Probation and Aftercare Department will give all particulars. In this field there are also training opportunities for suitable applicants up to the age of forty-nine as prison officers. Details are available from H.M. Prison Commission.

The National Society for the Prevention of Cruelty to Children runs one-year training courses starting twice a year in January and July, mainly in London. Trainees receive a lodging allowance and fares home at intervals, as well as pay while training. Candidates must be between twenty-five and forty-four. No special qualifications other than general suitability for the course and for the work are required. Applications should be made to the Secretary, N.S.P.C.C.

Three-day full-time courses are held at the Royal Institute of Public Health and Hygiene, 28 Portland Place, London W1, and part-time courses are held at over 100 other centres on Food Hygiene and the Handling of Food, leading to a certificate examination. The Institute also runs courses in General Hygiene, School Hygiene, Mothercraft and Child Welfare, and will send further details on request.

The Youth Service is likely to be one which will appeal to many widowed mothers and to those women who have a particular understanding of young people. There is a considerable shortage of women for this work, and those who prefer to work voluntarily in order to gain some experience should make inquiries through the Youth Officer for the town or borough in which they live. The minimum age of entry is twenty-three. Information on training is available from the National College for the Training of Youth Leaders. The course is for one year. Some universities have one-year courses too, and although these may vary they are usually recognized by local authorities both for grant aid while training and for appointments following training. There are some part-time courses.

Several aspects of youth work which may be of interest to women cover welfare officers in colleges, young people's advisers and moral welfare work. It is an advantage for welfare officers to have a social science qualification, but this is not essential. The main duty of such people is to visit approved lodgings, create good relationships between landladies and students and keep in touch with students' advisory bodies and with the British Council. The work is full time and could include evening work. Pay is good. Contact should be made with the local education authority department regarding possible appointments. Young people's advisers work sessionally and candidates should have some training in social work, teaching or youth work. Another service, which deals mainly with unmarried mothers, also requires social science qualifications and some practical experience of social service. In some cases it may be possible for women to get work without the basic social science degree or diploma, but it is usually considered advisable that they should have the Josephine Butler Diploma. This work too has the advantage of being part-time. The Church of England Social Responsibility Department is the organization to approach. The Family Service Units, which began as a voluntary body, now pay their caseworkers, who must have professional social work qualifications. This work is mainly with problem families.

Those who are interested in the possibility of either returning to or taking up nursing will know of the great need for nurses. If they are already qualified as state registered nurses they should have little difficulty in re-establishing themselves in their old profession. For those without the qualifications there are the following possibilities:

1. A two-year full-time course for state enrolment No educational certificate is required for this and candidates are selected for their suitability for the training and the work. Application must be made to the Nursing Recruitment Service for hospitals having those courses in the area in which the candidate wishes to train, or to the Regional Hospital Board. This training is now available in hospitals for the mentally ill as well as in a few hospitals for the mentally subnormal. There is a limited number of part-time training schemes for state enrolled nurses.

2. Two-year courses in midwifery for the mature woman No previous nursing experience and no special qualifications are required, but candidates are selected for suitability for the training and the work. Application should be made to the Royal College of Midwives. The training courses are usually resident, and for state-enrolled nurses the training period is reduced to eighteen months.

3. *Auxiliary nursing*   For this no training is needed, but selection of candidates with plenty of common sense is the rule. The nursing auxiliary helps the trained staff in the care of patients and does not do domestic work. There is no qualification at the end of a period of work of any length of time, so that those intending to continue auxiliary nursing should consider the state enrolment course. The nursing officer at the local hospital is the right person to approach.

4. *Ward aids*   Some hospitals need women in this capacity, to relieve the trained staff of non-nursing duties—that is, to answer the telephone, give out post, help new patients to settle in, arrange the flowers, check that notes, X-rays, etc., are ready for doctors' rounds. Part-time work is possible but the duties start at about 8.30 a.m. as this is the busiest time of the day in the wards.

The work of a Health Visitor can often be fitted into the life of a mother running a home and children more easily than work centred on a hospital. Training courses are available both for those who are already qualified SRN's and those who are not, and the experience of domestic and family life which a widow can bring to the work can be a real advantage.

For those who are looking for more domestic pursuits there is the Home Help Service, which is now well established throughout the country and is run by the local public health department. There are two kinds of work here, either as home help organizers or as home helps. No specific qualifications are needed for the organizers, but they are chosen for their obvious qualities of character and their domestic acumen and organizing abilities. Home helps must obviously be good at domestic work and they need to be fit and able women since they must go to homes often in a bad condition where there is much need of their service. Rates of pay vary according to local authorities. For anyone who is free to consider the venture, Home Help (Overseas) Ltd, of 35 George Street, Oxford, arrange jobs in Canada and elsewhere for mothers' helps, nannies and housekeepers.

In many households emergencies can occur which demand an able woman housekeeper for a long or short period. There are jobs of various kinds available through, amongst others, the Over Forty Association, Universal Aunts and the Employment Fellowship. A number of less well-known services have sprung up to cover this need, some good and some not so reliable. An enterprising woman with business knowledge and aptitude can start such an organization herself locally, provided she knows enough women who will be willing to give their practical support. This can prove something of a difficulty, but there are those who have made a success of it. If widows wish to do domestic work of this emergency kind the pay is good (about £14 a week and all found) and the work is liable to be fairly short term so that they need not consider giving up their homes and can return to their personal independence. Cruse has a list of organizations and agencies of this kind.

Work which may interest women with a natural aptitude for the managerial side of domestic skills is that of institution management. One-year courses for older women with study and practical training can lead to interesting posts in different types of institutions. Application should be made to the Institutional Management Association, who will give details of courses in various parts of the country. Local education authority grants can sometimes be secured to cover this training. Staff for the catering trade, both part- and full-time and resident, are in great demand, and you should apply to the Hotel and Catering Institute for general information. Some local authorities run special courses for older women as cooks. Vacancies are in hotels, restaurants and canteens. Hotels may offer accommodation too, and this could in some cases include a child.

A management career in Marks & Spencer has many possibilities but promotion may take women to other parts of the country. For sales staff of age nineteen and over the starting salary is generous for a five-day week (some Saturdays). Part-time staff are welcomed and are paid by the hour. There is often an excellent staff restaurant for lunch and a staff hairdressing salon. Details can be obtained from the Staff Manageress. Other large concerns such as the oil companies offer an extensive range of work of many kinds, from computer development to primary school teaching abroad and copy or audio typing.

Very understandably the care of children has great appeal for many women and the following suggestions cover much of this field of work. Untrained women wishing to become child care officers must be over twenty-five and preferably under forty-five. There is the possibility of financial help during training and courses take two years for those without a social science qualification but with kindred training in teaching or health visiting. There are also two-year courses for older women who have not obtained the necessary qualifications required for entrance to a university, but who have a sufficiently high standard of general education to benefit from the training. Application should be made to the Central Training Council in Child Care.

House-parent courses for work in local authority children's homes are also available at certain centres, and application should be made direct to the chosen area. There is financial help during training. Responsible work which can be undertaken without any form of training is fostering and child-minding. Fostering is certainly not well paid, but there is a great need for women who will take children for from a few weeks to the whole period of childhood. Arrangements are made through the public health department, children's department, or privately. Child-minding includes the care of children at any time of the day in the child-minder's home, but does not cover sleeping overnight. The public health department must be approached if more than two children, or three of one family, are being cared for. Registration is then necessary and relates to the suitability of the person doing the child-minding and the premises in which this is to be done.

Women who enjoy caring for old people and who like their company may want to use their homes for this worth-while work. Only those with nursing experience should undertake care of the infirm, and the public health department should be informed. The elderly who are lonely when their families have left them often look for unfurnished or furnished rooms with some service and companionship. Given a warm and suitably built house this can be a new extension of the home, helping the widow-owner financially and creating a community for elderly people who need it. The advertisement columns of *The Lady* and other weekly or national papers are helpful in making contacts.

Many women have found great satisfaction in work for the subnormal and mentally handicapped. This is a special field with openings for the right people whether qualified or not. Details can be obtained from the National Association for Mental Health and from the Training Council for Teachers of the Mentally Handicapped.

Other groups urgently needing help are the blind, the deaf and the disabled. The Royal National Institute for the Blind gives one-year part-time training to home teachers of embossed type reading, handicrafts and social activities. Applications for work with the deaf or disabled should be sent to the College of Deaf Welfare and to the British Council for the Rehabilitation of the Disabled. Help is often needed in the Cheshire Homes.

There are many opportunities for work in schools on the domestic side either as teaching auxiliaries part time or as resident matrons. Sometimes a widow's children may be accepted as well in residential posts. Write to Gabbitas-Thring Educational Trust.

Work in industry is beginning to offer more opportunities for part-time work for women. Those who must work restricted hours should remain alert to changes in attitude in big firms where many staff are employed and a welcome is sometimes offered to those who can work part time, or who are willing to undertake shifts. Local inquiries should be made through the Employment Exchange or direct to the personnel officer of any large firm. Personnel management in commerce and industry is an interesting line for women and, although academic qualifications are desirable, personal qualities and past experience are taken into account. There are part-time courses at some technical colleges for those with industrial experience. Information is available from the Institute of Personnel Management.

Chiropody is work which appeals to some women, and there are seven or eight schools of chiropody in the country, including two in London, one each in Glasgow, Edinburgh, Manchester and Leicester. The educational qualifications for entry are a minimum of four 'O' levels, and the course takes three years. This is a worthwhile and lasting career which also offers special opportunities for encouraging and helping older people, who use this service a great deal. Details can be obtained from the Society of Chiropodists.

Horticulture is becoming more and more popular with women, and there is now a two-year course which can be taken at Nottingham, Reading and London Universities. One year's practical work must be done before applying for the course, and a minimum educational requirement is five 'O' levels with at least one of them in a science subject. There are one-year courses available sometimes at further education centres. The work covers research, landscape design, experimental work, garden management and maintenance, and nursery and commercial horticulture. Jobs can sometimes be secured abroad.

What is termed 'outwork' really means work for a firm done in the home and is popular with many housebound women. For example, corsetry outwork is often available for suitably trained women for two to three days a week. The Clothing Institute will give details. Other outwork may cover typing, needlework, clothes-making, assembly of parts and lampshade making, etc. It is usually badly paid and may be exceedingly monotonous. It may also be unpleasant in some feature or take up a great deal of room to the annoyance of other family members. Advertisements for this type of work may be found in the main evening, weekly and local newspapers. Special care is advised where attractive prospects are held out for work in the home on condition that a machine is bought from the firm. These are often 'selling tricks' and should be regarded with caution. Offers of work once the machine is bought and the operator reasonably proficient may add up to nothing.

There is no doubt that special situations arise either where a widow must earn money at once, or where she must use initiative and imagination in a difficult local setting. I suggest some possibilities without adding detail beyond saying that some such jobs are advertised in, for example, sweet shops or newsagents', and others may be run to earth by advertising under a box number in the local shop. Occasionally a church or meeting house noticeboard might prove helpful. It is important to state charges per hour in your advertisement and standard rates should be given. If these are not known the matter could be discussed with the Citizens' Advice Bureau in your nearest town. The book *Retire and Enjoy It* has a useful appendix giving chapter and verse on how to go about starting work of this kind and giving details of equipment which may be needed, although the prices and possible earnings should be further checked with current figures. Gardening by the hour (especially for elderly people); washing up in cafés or hotels; amateur decorating; baby walking or minding; caring for animals or birds in the owner's absence; dog walking or minding; teaching English to foreigners; mending house linen or socks;

turning up skirts, dresses or coats (basic rates for this work are listed at cleaners); sitting with or shopping for invalids or elderly people; pushing out invalids in wheelchairs (this may be heavy work); cooking evening meals; keeping chickens or ducks; breeding budgies, pedigree dogs or cats; making small souvenirs for sale in tourist centres; child or animal photography; running a paper round with a car or moped, are all ideas which could be followed up. The widow selling her services should prepare duplicated lists of prices covering the different services offered. Without this she will find that people will readily take all she will give for no recompense, as so many lack the imagination to grasp the difficulties of her financial position. For those who are free to be away for a few months, acting as hostess for a travel agency abroad, or for a house party at home, can be fun. Organizers of distribution teams are always wanted, as well as those who do the door-to-door distribution of leaflets and advertising literature. Marketforce Ltd of 97 Dalston Lane, London E.8, will tell you what opportunities there are in your area. Incidentally, occupations and trades for which registration or licences are required include beautician, chiropodist, dancing and music teaching, employment agency, hairdresser, massage, nursing home, petshop, boarding kennels, taxi service.

In Chapter 7 I have dealt with ways of making your house work for you. If you prefer to take foreign visitors into your home and have reasonable amenities, you can both enjoy their company, speak another language and get better payment. The usual figure is from £11 a week with breakfast, supper and week-end meals. The great advantage is that there are lower heating expenses in the summer months and visitors pay their own contribution on excursions. Or if an all-in figure is arranged, your expenses as guide can be included. On such occasions it would possibly be expected that you would provide picnic lunch. Foreign guests can much enliven the house, and arrangements to be a host family can be made by writing to the British Council, the En Famille Agency, or to the Anglo-Scandinavian Educational Holidays.

If you are very enterprising you may wish to start a business, although you should remember that you will probably have to have a licence from your local authority or county council. It may be necessary also to register for tax purposes, or your business name or trademark. Cruse has a Fact Sheet on 'Buying a Business'.

A number of women have been successful in working for mail-order companies as agents, receiving a commission of around two shillings in the pound on sales. Selling about £1,000 worth of goods a year will yield only £2 a week at this rate, and you may consider this is not an adequate return for the time spent. To raise more than this per week would require a large circle of customers, and the widow must be sure that she will have this before embarking on such work. There are a number of mail-order companies, but inquiries could be directed to Littlewoods in the first place.

Probably any plans you think of will make you aware of practical difficulties: having to leave the house empty, being out when your children return from school, coping with the expected run of children's infectious illnesses when they are young, giving up pets which cannot be left, shopping in working hours, preparing and cooking meals, washing, ironing, mending, cleaning and gardening—all these aspects of home life must be considered too. So must your own physical stamina as a working mother or as a woman now living alone. Elsewhere in this book I have suggested ways of economizing in time, money and effort. Certainly a new set of priorities is essential if you are to keep your health and contentment under the strain of the double role of mother and breadwinner. Any training you undertake will be well worth while even if it stretches you considerably at the time. Your rewards come later, in personal fulfilment, satisfying relationships, a sense of being needed in the community and, last but not least, the knowledge that you have paid your way.

I and my children alone

What a father is—Children and death—On not being involved—Hardening off in the nursery—Children can't explain—A father's existence is not the same as his survival—Understanding a child's grief—The internal image of the father is forgiven—Being naughty is natural—Mothers can be too close—There are people who can help—The mother opens doors—Enriching family life—Helping in the home—Family conference—Sex and the children—Yes or no to boarding school—Your men friends—Further education and work—Mother remarries—Going on alone.

To be well fathered is to belong, to feel safe, to know the ground of life is secure. It is to know that father is able to control that part of the world which is his, be it counting milk bottles, healing people or building bridges. Best of all it is to feel enfolded in a relationship where mother is too and where she also is secure. Of course it is many other things too. Father is the fountainhead of wisdom, the encyclopaedia with the answer to all the 'whys'. He is the great big comfortable bear to roll with, to ride on. He is the haven of every return from adventure. He is the big to the small, the strong to the weak. He is the man of all seasons, the magic bridge into the exciting, frightening world. Life without him is unthinkable. He goes, but he always comes again. He comes when things are dark and muddled, when anger rises in clouds to hide the sun. He brings too that fair judgment which understands the self-punishment of failure and stays to make things new and whole again.

So we could see the true role of the father in the mind of the child—the maleness in man. To acknowledge that countless men fall short of their children's view of them, or indeed of their needs, in no way dims this deep awareness of their significance. In its understanding we begin to see the grief of a deprived child. Such grief may come in many situations, and not by any means only through death. A father can have so many ways of 'going'. He may leave the mother's life, he may leave her heart, he may go to war, he may travel far away, he may break up the home for another woman, but if he goes by death his 'desertion' is complete. The game of soldiers has become a terrible reality, the captain of the force has gone for good. The baby's game of 'peek-a-boo' has become a nightmare of truth. Who can now understand the terror in the night, the great waste land of loss? You who are a child are so little, so helpless, so wholly unprotected in the great big world.

In the mind of the child death is always a mystery. It is a 'falling down', a 'falling apart like the flowers', a 'going to sleep altogether'; 'the invisible part of you is left'; 'it's when your blood has run out'; 'it's when you're very old, or killed in war, or drowned'; 'it's when you have no strength'; 'death isn't like sleep—it's for ever', 'when you can't feel any more thoughts'; 'they die when the death man catches them'; 'their bodies hung like grotesque rag dolls on the barbed wire'; 'its feathers were so soft and blue but it didn't move in my hand'; 'they flung the stiff bodies into the lorry —they didn't seem like animals any more—they were like boards'; 'he looked so much smaller, not a bit frightening. They had put a little white silk rose on his forehead—it was silly'. So children of all ages have talked of death.

There are other kinds of loss too, causing immediate overwhelming distress or hurts that are never shared: the dearly loved doll or teddy, somehow completely part of the little child; the very special stone—the thing which has magic and is part of a fantasy life which is utterly real; the playfellow who goes away to another town; the friendship which is broken; the loved home, the secret place—all these are subjects for mourning when we lose them. They are the wounds that life inflicts, but none is so shattering as the death of the parent, because a child's whole life is changed. Nothing is ever quite the same again. There can be no replacement of the one who was part of the self.

The emotions stirred by this experience are very mixed and children often show their confusion—a confusion seen too in the mother who is shocked and grieving. If there are many children the older ones will be able to support the little ones. Much will depend on which sex they are, or where they come in the sibling group, on their closeness to the father, on the character and emotional stability of the mother. All will have their own guilt feeling—'If only I had not done so and so', 'If only I had understood and helped more', 'I didn't really mean it when I wished him dead in that row we had'. For the little child the natural growth of individuality, the fight for identity, the demand for a place in the adult world, even those difficult moments when father is seen as the rival for mother; all these feelings, so right in their context, now seem to be betrayed by death and the 'going away'. There is too the complexity of relationship with mother, the feeling that there is now only one 'rightness', not two. Suddenly rivalry with the other children has a new painfulness. The child who was especially close to father is exposed before the others. Mother's favourite child is in a privileged position but at the same time lost and insecure because she has become so too. The child at war with father, struggling for independence, is pulled in two directions: glad that he is gone, ashamed to be glad, and afraid of the secret. There can be a rivalry over mourning—who cares most—who is to show it—child or mother? A newly bereaved family is indeed a house of confusion, perhaps outwardly united, but inwardly each member is seething with a private emotion which waits to be resolved.

In the British way of life there has developed in the last century a growing dislike of display of feeling—a technique of non-involvement. This can be and has been encouraged from top to bottom of the social pattern of behaviour so that gradually what is emotive becomes stifled. The taboo on revealing emotion may begin early. To shed tears is 'girlish', to be 'one of the boys' is good. The training starts early, and the mothers and fathers of today have been printed indelibly with its pattern. Psychiatrists tell us that mothers are largely responsible, checking the warmth and sensitivity of their boys, joining in the plans for 'hardening off young plants' of the nursery. Nowhere is this clearer than in boarding-school life, especially if this starts before a child has the ego strength to stand alone. However much security the home may or may not have in mother/father relationship, to be parcelled off when the three Rs are barely learned is a deprivation akin to bereavement. It is a pattern of experience which has much to do with the British stiff upper lip and the fear of feeling. The lesson has been so well learned that social workers and professional analysts are now telling us that we must 'do our grief work' if we are to be mentally healthy. The stages of grief are laid down for us. 'Permission to grieve' is offered in the respectable context of social service. Of this our children are hardly aware as they struggle amongst the confused emotions of their elders, sometimes seeing them with a clarity and simplicity which shame us. As they deal with the taboos they have inherited they too must find the way.

Many widowed mothers understand this, and some, because they have rejected emotion, have shown the world a proud and angry face, protecting their children with a fierce care. It is an aspect of widowhood that is real. Some have lost the mother in themselves, others have found it in a new depth of tenderness, a new friendship with their children. Some can say with truth that this is a growth point in living when a woman may find a new strength in herself. Grief nevertheless is real and its pain has no antidote. It is there to be borne in the night and in the day, whether in the measure of a woman's experience or of a child's.

The hurt animal and the hurt child have much in common. 'Where is the pain?' says the doctor. 'What is it like?' Children can't explain, and this much must be understood by deduction or by the memory of what it was to be a child. What we do know is that with the death of the father the structure of the family is greatly disturbed and that, try as she may, a woman cannot be a substitute for a man. Were she to try, her child then lacks a mother too. Dr Donald Winnicott has distinguished between the importance of the father's existence and his survival, which, he says, are not the same. Of the father's existence he says: 'First of all there is the stabilizing effect on the family and on the mother. There is the feeling of being able to depend on the father. When he goes the child has, at least for a time, a depressed, grief-stricken mother, one who is deeply disturbed. She who could cope now finds it difficult.

'It is as though a small boy were playing "mothers and fathers" in which he happily takes the fantasy father role. Suddenly the fantasy changes to reality—his father is dead and he finds he really is in the male "father" role. He is very frightened, becoming impotent because he realizes that in reality he is only a small child. He can no longer identify himself in fantasy with his parent as father,

husband or workman. Before he could be both a little child and all
these roles.

'Or there is the little girl of four who is having a "love affair"
with her father; they are tremendously close. It is private, and
happy, and secret, and yet quite safe because somehow everyone
knows and understands. It interweaves too with the mother's
function. When the father dies the mother and her little girl can
find themselves at war. There is almost a rivalry over grieving.
Someone in this situation will have to be very tolerant, very understanding.

'It is convenient to talk of boys and girls, because in our society
the differences are not always very clearly defined. Most boys
have a lot of the girl in them, and most girls have a lot of the boy.
In some societies the differences are made very clear: boys are
boys and identified with the male role, girls are girls and identified
with the mothers and grandmothers. In a family of several children the tensions may be very mixed.'

Of the father's survival, Dr Winnicott says: 'I believe the most
important job of parents is to survive. To be there. This is especially important over the puberty years where aggressive ideas are
being dealt with by the child. They both love and hate. They have
destructive ideas, which may come in nightmares. It is very
important when the child has dreamed his father's death that this
dream should not come true in reality. Such aggressive thoughts,
and we all have and have had them, are too dangerous if they
become real. Should this happen the child must inhibit feeling because of this danger. So it becomes withdrawn, seeming not to
care, shallow in its behaviour. In this thing survival the father has
failed the child. Of course he could not help it, but this is how it is
for the child. His fantasy world is destroyed. It has become reality.
When this happens depression often follows.

'What can we say of the fact of death? One who was alive is now
dead. He is gone for ever; but there is something important that
goes on. This is the image of the father in the child. It is a live
image which was and is always being knocked down and being put
up again—just like a toy soldier. This is where the reassurance of
the reality father is so important. He always comes back. If he is
away for some weeks the child will manage all right, but if he is
away for some years it is as though the child no longer has a father
—he has, as it were, "died off" in the child. The man who comes

back is another man, he is no longer his father. If he has "died off" in the mother too it is very difficult indeed for the child.

'The death of this internal image of the loved person may bring depression, but in time it may come alive again. It is as though it becomes "forgiven". "Alive" moments are remembered. The child can "stand the father up again". Of course it is easier for him if the mother can do the same. Should the mother turn to another man this may give the child some relief. He no longer feels the responsibility for keeping his mother happy. Children often feel they must not be happy if the mother is not. Most of us are guilty over other people's unhappiness and loss. We feel this about widows. What right have we to be happy when the widow is unhappy? Suppose the same thing happened to us?'

To see the father's role in the life of a child is to see possible ways in which bereaved children can be helped. It is this the widowed mother wants to know about. Deep in herself she knows how bad the blow to her children is, but if she is wise in the real sense of wisdom she knows that nature has its healing ways.

In growing up all children need to match their aggression against the grown-up world. This is equally true for the widow's child, if more difficult for her to manage alone. Being angry, being naughty, being physically aggressive are preparation for the battles of life. In these feelings, and in their control, a child finds its measure, and the emotion is at the same time contained in safety. If we destroy aggressive impulses without understanding their true value we may destroy growth points in the personality which are essential to all endeavour in adult life. A boy must establish his defiance, do battle with the father, until he can take his place in society on his own. Every healthy boy from eleven to fourteen gets into scrapes, swearing, stealing, fighting, or what you will. This is when the father or father figure is needed, not to condemn but to understand and put the youngster back on the path. The father is the bridge to adult life as a man. Some families invoke the authority of the Church, and God may even become the 'Spying Eye', the policeman or the man with a big stick. So often this is how people later on come to throw out the valuable asset of a true religious belief. Fortunately the medieval concept of hell-fire has for the great majority gone the way of other inquisitorial patterns of control.

In the growing-up of boys there may be over-attachment to the mother but, when the father is there and significant in her life, this is brought into balance. Without him the widow can need guidance over the handling of her sons. Winston Churchill, one of the great figures of our time, was for an important period of his life a widow's child. He writes tellingly of the experience; 'Solitary trees, if they grow at all, grow strong; and a boy deprived of a father's care often develops, if he escapes the perils of youth, an independence and vigour of thought which may restore in after life the heavy loss of early days.' True for him, it is unhappily not so for all. Sometimes one boy only takes the brunt of a widow's deprived emotions. He is the one who may never marry or who philanders through the years because of his unresolved attachment to his mother.

When the family is in early bereavement the mother should not hesitate to talk about the father's death with the children. Denying the fact of it is far more harmful, and anyway children have their own fantasies, as we have indicated. Tears are healing and no one should fear them. Grief driven underground has its dangers, and both mother and children should be encouraged to talk of the father, his life, his ways and even his weaknesses. It is all part of the healing process which, after all, comes from inside the one who mourns, whether child or adult.

Bereavement response in children which is clear to those who care for them should give us our warning light. The child who was happy and manageable suddenly goes wild, is almost uncontrollable at school; the lively child becomes quiet and withdrawn and no longer looks for friends; any reference to the father is rigorously avoided and the child will leave the room if the subject comes up. At school all concentration in lessons is gone, the child formerly at the top is now at the bottom of the class, exams are failed. Explosive, and it may be destructive, anger follows every failure in achievement. The church-going youngsters refuse to go any more. A boy starts stealing, a little one takes money from the mother's purse. Nightmares come. Asthma, never apparent before, bedwetting and a return to baby behaviour suddenly appear. There is the hunger of a little girl for every 'daddy' figure, sometimes most embarrassing to the mother. These and many other signs of disturbance in their children are known to widows. What can be done?

First the mother needs to find her own equilibrium, and she will not necessarily do better by pretending she can manage alone when she could help herself by accepting support, however temporary. To stand by a bereaved mother is often to support her children. And you who are in this position need all the available wisdom there is. It is unlikely to be a road you know. At the Child Guidance Clinic there are doctors and social workers who understand and with whom you yourself can discuss the right handling of your children at this difficult time. If anything baffles you, use the people who have studied the emotional life of children. If school work is the problem a sympathetic staff may not be enough and you may need the educational psychologist. If you can cope, but feel the weight and loneliness of being a mother on your own, join other widowed mothers and see how they deal with the situation. It can be most heartening to know how others manage. You can read about this in Cruse Parents' Circle Reports. They have a range of literature too, especially prepared for the widowed mother, including the booklet *The Widow's Child*. 'Gingerbread' is an association for one-parent families. It is run by members from their homes, and the best way to find out if there is a group in your locality is to ask at the library, or the Citizens' Advice Bureau. 'Mothers in Action' is linked to Gingerbread, and covers those with children who want to bring about various changes to benefit families and help each other.

Some of you have tried to look into a future with no father for your children and have felt deeply apprehensive. At such times it helps to help yourself first, as your child's security rests on yours. Within the situation we know there is healing too, because other widows have found this. What matters is that you should not shut doors but open them. Aim at making your home a warm and welcoming place for your children and their friends. Let them know their relatives better too, form a closer relationship with grandparents, uncles and aunts, while keeping your hold on the situation. Be a 'joiner' yourself and encourage the children to join clubs and groups known for their good and happy handling of youngsters together. Encourage them to try new activities and don't encourage too exclusive friendships. Make and keep 'whole family' relationships and help when you can. Try to give others the benefit of the doubt. If their goodwill does not always overflow it is probably nothing to do with you, and over-sensitivity will help no one—least of all yourself. Your life is not an easy one now, but you can live with a young spirit. Before you fully realize it you can be living with, and accepting, challenge in a new way, Most of all the children will thank you for this.

Of course your money is short and you have to scheme and plan. The children won't really suffer from this unless you are always harping on money problems. Sit down one day and get your family priorities right. First look after the health of all of you. See that the children sleep enough. Plan a good diet for the family, and talk it over with the children so that they know why some foods are a 'must' and accept the family menus. See that all of you have right and enjoyable exercise and outdoor pursuits. If you can, run a Saturday club for the children and their friends, most of whom will have two parents, and soon you will have other parents co-operating. Fathers will take the club on special jaunts. I recall one such wonderful visit to an airfield where the youngsters even talked down a plane; and you should try to get help with fishing, carpentry, football and other activities. Mothers may help with museum visits and holiday interests and you won't be doing it all alone for long, as this is a real community need for many fathers and mothers, especially where mothers go out to work. If you can swim, ride, sail or water-ski you can soon get a group of children round you. There will be teaching to do and you will soon find that week-ends become richer and more worth while. Pantomime and theatre parties 'in the gods' at Christmas can give great enrichment at a difficult time too.

You will hear some say that they can't afford to entertain either their children's friends or their own any more. Informality is the key here. Have a candle party with bread and cheese or sausage rolls, a one-dish (preferably a foreign recipe with a good name!) supper with fruit to follow for older friends. Invite children for a special mid-morning snack over the week-end. You can make quite an institution of it. The great thing is to give the occasion a feeling of difference and no one will notice if you have spent very little money on it. Keep away from formality and you can soon cut down costs. Enterprising mothers may want to make 'country' wines to lay by for occasions too. If you're thinking of going to London or on an 'expedition' try to take some other children too, and take lunch in rucksacks so that you have both hands free for your young companions. If you want to know where to go get a copy of *What's on In London for Young People* and *Nicholson's*

London Guide, and let them share in making up the programme. Have a good map with you and teach yourself and them how to use it. All this will be a step to the day when they want to go alone with friends on a Red Rover bus ticket.

If you yourself can bear to be without television you may find, as so many others have, that communication between members of the family becomes more fun. Sitting, and not doing, is a poor alternative to shared activities and reading together. Get the children their own library tickets, even if you are not a reader, so that they get the fun of reading books of their own choice and going to the library by themselves. The older ones can soon learn to use the reference library too. You are sure to have a radio, and even if you have a television set too, make an occasion of marking the programmes when the papers come so that you really do watch and listen to programmes on current affairs, travel, theatre, poetry, book discussions and other interesting items. The school programmes too can be fascinating for adults. Try to avoid quarrelling over which programme is to be on.

There are many practical decisions to make. What jobs in the home and garden can the children take on? You can't do it all. How much pocket money can you spare for them? Ought they to do Saturday jobs? As soon as you can, start a little family conference, have it regularly and see that everyone is there. Have a complaints item on the agenda every time and really talk it over! Decide if members of the family ought to learn special domestic skills and see that they have help from you, a friend or relative in learning. A boy should know how to mend his socks, put on buttons, press his trousers and iron a shirt. A girl should know how to mend a fuse, put up a shelf, drive a nail straight. Both need to know how to cook a basic meal and have the elements of good diet in their mind. If your daughter can't sew and cut out see that she learns, perhaps with you. This skill especially will help to give her up-to-the-minute clothes. Your sons may want to learn more than cutting grass in the garden, and you can both learn about taking cuttings, grafting, pruning and raising vegetables. These are all wonderful skills to use all your life. Make your garden a family interest too. Give the little ones their own plot. We discuss garden care in another chapter.

Going to school is for many children a hard discipline. Your best plan is to know your children's schools and staffs well. When they know you are bringing your family up without a father they will take a special interest in your children. Never miss a Parents' Day if possible; send a relative if you can't go. Be active in any parent-teacher group.

Don't be over anxious if after their father's death the children lose heart in their work. It often happens. Given time the children will recover; seek help if they don't. Remember that in all stress situations in exams, friendships and school problems your child will need extra support.

See that sex matters are understood reasonably early and where possible talked about openly. Cruse have a range of booklets for different ages. Your family doctor may be the best to deal with your son's sex development, and will usually give time if you ask. He too will say what should be said about homosexual difficulties. What matters is to cope with questions from boys and girls when they come up and give replies without going into lengthy descriptions of procreation which were not asked for. See that your girls are clear about menstruation, pregnancy and venereal disease, and tell them that for most girls having a baby outside marriage will only ruin all their fun and their future. They especially will know what it means for a child to be without a father. In this context you may find your children have views about any men friends you have. As long as they are protected and feel that you are loved and cared for by your friends they will welcome them. They may be jealous too, but this will depend on the kind of relationship you have with the children. Usually they want you to be happy and will be relieved when you are. A man who makes you unhappy they can come to hate. Of course you will be careful about allowing older men to give presents to your young daughters and be sure there are no strings attached. Presents, you can tell them, are not 'for services rendered'. That kind are best rejected. Warn them quite simply about not taking lifts from strangers.

If you take young foreigners into your house they will need supervision, as indeed they are used to this at home. Freedom in Britain can be heady wine for some of them. Where smoking, drinking and drugs are concerned, these should go on your family conference agenda on a suitable occasion. Get the facts and give them to your children in terms of hard cash and of health hazards.

If you can go on 'interest' holidays with the children where there are other families, you can be more sure of a happy time.

Choose house party or family holidays where all of you can make new relationships and be a little free of each other at times. For holidays the whole family should save and plan together. Cruse has a comprehensive Holiday List full of ideas for the fatherless family.

Quite soon you may all feel that the house could serve you better in its arrangement. You may want to turn all your rooms into bed-sitting rooms to which each of you can retreat at times. You may have to sacrifice one room for a paying guest. Your kitchen could be converted into a buffet dining-room. As long as you have one 'together' room the family will be united part of the time. Have a lean-to workshop for your boys if you cannot afford a shed, and have a bench put up. For small children a 'Wendy house' might be the perfect gift to enrich their relationship with friends. It may also make your house quieter if you have paying guests.

Considering the decision to send your child to boarding school, it is generally accepted that children need the support of the home until puberty, and may suffer emotionally in being sent away to school too early. Every parent of a child at boarding school is aware that this can be an experience of considerable stress, especially to the sensitive and imaginative type of child. Very much will depend on the school. There are ample records in biographies to indicate the problems in some of our best-known boarding schools, where the 'toughening' process is regarded as salutary. A widow's child is often already insecure, and greatly fears the loss of its mother. If you have a clear choice and are able to offer a fully supporting home life with relatives, or permanent mother's help, you probably will not be likely to choose a boarding school for your child. A weekly boarding school may offer a good compromise, provided it is reasonably near the home. If, on the other hand, you are finding difficulty in maintaining the home, are economically much pressed, must train for work or undertake long hours in earning, or if you have problems in controlling a high-spirited son, you may feel that boarding school is the right decision. The choice may then depend on where foundations or bursaries are to be found. Cruse has a Boarding School list offering useful suggestions. Difficult as it is, there certainly are instances where the supportive care of a boarding school has saved a child from becoming a major problem. If this has already happened your local education authority may advise sending the child to boarding school and in this case will meet the fees at a school chosen by them to suit your child's need. Many child care experts recognize the value of the co-educational boarding school where 'father' and 'mother' figures abound and the natural 'big family' atmosphere is achieved. The presence of other children without fathers can be a good thing, as it can help a child to realize that it is not alone in this special experience. If you feel real difficulty in making a decision after reviewing the position from all angles, you may wish to talk over the pros and cons with the educational psychologist, a sympathetic 'Head' or a social worker who knows you and your family.

There are special burdens some widows must carry and others they create themselves. If you are a mother whose child was born after its father's death you will feel real heartache for the baby who must grow up without its father. You have one comfort in that your little one has not to bear bereavement as little children must when they lose their father. Your difficulty will rather be in establishing the male image in the inner life of your child. Somehow this needs to be done or an unreal fantasy thinking may develop. It will be even more important for this child to have a father substitute.

An especially difficult situation can come about if your husband was mentally ill and ended his life. Here both you and your children will need to find that growth point of forgiveness from which all of you can go on. To talk the whole matter out for your own understanding is vitally important, and if the children have emotional difficulties you are well advised to go to the specialists at the Child Guidance Clinic. Here your children can find 'fathers' on whom to project their emotion and come to healing in themselves. You have to remember that, however sensible you may be in what you say, your children have to contend with public attitudes in the neighbourhood, amongst relatives and with the remarks of their schoolfellows.

One of the deepest fears of your children is that something will happen to you. About this you can do little but look after your health, insure if you wish against emergencies, and have your will made and safely put away with directions regarding the care of your children by guardians you have chosen for them. Better still, see that the children have a relationship with their guardians and that they have plenty of friends. If you have a child suffering a disability of any kind you will be all the more concerned that provision is made. Here too take the support of those organizations specially qualified to give it. If these matters are more or less settled in your mind you will yourself project a feeling of security to your children.

Finally, try not to fall into the trap of leaning too heavily on your son, as some widows do, taking first his childhood from him and then, if you are not very careful, turning him into a husband substitute. If you, perhaps unconsciously, develop a too close emotional relationship with him you will strip some of his manhood and he will have the greatest difficulty in taking a sustained male role in marriage. Indeed he may never marry while you live. Even at the risk of leaving some jobs undone, or doing them yourself and quite often being lonely, avoid this situation at all costs. There have been far too many men ruined by the emotional demands of their mothers. Something not unlike this can happen between a widowed mother and her daughter, creating a battleground of feelings which can tear them apart. In any case a girl who has lost her father at an early age can have a special problem in relation to men. She may choose in a husband a father figure to give her the security she has lacked, or she may so long for male companionship that she makes unwise or shallow relationships, lacking in true judgment.

One of the most difficult problems you as a mother alone have to face is the sexual development of your children in the teens. You may carry along most happily until the complications burst round you. Then you will feel the need to get things straight in your own thinking. Basically the problems relate to the changing behaviour patterns of our time. So much appeared simple when it was said, categorically, that masturbation is naughty or bad, sex exploration is dirty, a girl's menstruation and a boy's wet dreams are taboo subjects, intercourse is only for married people and is otherwise wicked. When all these ideas could be bolstered up with a firm religious teaching, a controlling army of parsons and priests and a powerful, punishing God, everything appeared to support them. This, however, is not how people think any more, with a few struggling exceptions, and the post-war generations really believe in their freedom to love and to express their love. Sex is seen as exciting and natural, and many are experiencing it early,

without consulting their parents. In fact to reject this way of freedom may mark a boy or girl as 'soft' or 'afraid'. You the mother
alone cannot hold back the tide, and you are in the difficult position of keeping alive a respect for the home which children
usually observe when father is there. You have to admit too that
the more they come to know about sex the more they will be aware
of your deprivation in this respect.

First of all then you must do all you can to ensure that your
daughters do not become pregnant and that your sons do not
make other girls so. Unless you can play on powerful guilt feelings
inculcated in your children's response to life before they were old
enough to think for themselves, you have only two good weapons
to use—your love for them and a clear and honest frankness. It is
no good being squeamish and 'shy'. If you are, your best plan is to
find some wise assistance soon. You may use all the explanatory
sex booklets available but you must still be willing to talk freely
and honestly. Many young people are choosing marriage partners
on the basis of a good deal of experimentation. It is in this period
that they need support, but you have a right to have your home,
and the behaviour in it, the way you want it. In fact if your children have a genuine respect for you they will want this too, especially as it is all you have, and they one day will want to feel that you
and the family support them in a happy marriage. For you this
matters a lot because grandchildren in a setting you can all accept
will mean so much happiness to all of you.

Should your children go to work straight from school you
should consider giving them the chance of a talk on contraception
with your doctor or an advisory clinic, assuming that they have
already had the basic explanations. You will probably know the
type of relationships they develop and it is no good reacting vio-
lently when it is too late. If they go to college it is probable that
their fellow students will give them all the knowledge they have
missed, and you may find that they begin sex relationship there
without any sense of guilt whatever. You may find too that your
daughter knows all about 'the pill', and there is nothing to stop
her going to a Brook Advisory Clinic on her own. So far as your
sons are concerned, until there is a male equivalent, they will use a
sheath for contraceptive and hygienic purposes. Even these, as
you know, are not a complete safeguard against making a girl
pregnant. If you are a Catholic both you and your children have

rules laid down on morality issues. Your children's difficulty will be to avoid the prevailing freedom amongst those not of your Church.

Many mothers will appreciate this appraisal of the situation, knowing that they will not serve their children's interests well if their silence or rejection of the subject leads to trouble. Being alone they have a special responsibility which must be recognized. A 'shot-gun' marriage is rarely the basis of a happy relationship and, provided advice is sought very soon after the menstrual period fails to appear, something can be done. The Pregnancy Advisory Service is there to help, and pregnancy tests anyhow can be done at advertised laboratories or by your family doctor. The wide publicity given nowadays to the problems of the unmarried mother and her illegitimate children leaves women very clear as to their unhappy position.

Looking ahead to school-leaving we have to admit that the days when a slap-happy attitude to work training could produce results are fast leaving us. Employers now, more than ever, want evidence of satisfactory school work, preferably in 'O' or 'A' levels, or willingness to train within a job. Your child cannot look for a father's support, financially or otherwise, and for this reason it is doubly important that maximum education and training should be taken in order to ensure a good career and a job with prospects. There is the added possibility that in their adult years you may need your children's help when you have used up your health, strength and means in allowing them further education rather than hurrying them out to earn with poor qualifications or none. It is you who know that easy money at the outset may well mean redundancy later on.

What then should you do to help your child at this time when decisions which may be far reaching must be taken? You are a fortunate mother if your children are quite clear about what they want to do. Many are not, and their school record may tell you nothing. You can be sure of one thing: most widows' children have a sharp experience of home economy, and this can either make them choose money above everything else or, if they are wise, a training which will give real security eventually. If they are left unsure of their futures, idling away time, and very probably taking social security, they and you are likely to be most unhappy. This possibility will have been brought to the notice of every youngster who leaves school without a job to go to, as they must sign on at the Employment Exchange if they are to receive state aid in the interval.

So a good deal of time and thought given well in advance by your children, school staff, the Youth Employment Officer and such advisory bodies as are available will pay dividends. If you can reach no satisfactory conclusion you may be glad to spend the money on a vocational guidance test. There are thirty Occupational Guidance units set up by the Department of Employment and Productivity in different parts of the country. The service is free. The Careers Research and Advisory Centre gives individual advice for a small fee. In all these it can be a good plan to book through Cruse if you are a member as there may be the possibility of financial support or a reduced fee. The Advisory Centre for Education is a useful organization to know if you want objective comment on school or further education plans. There is a small fee.

In the meantime there are reference books to study which will add information to what may or may not be gleaned through the school. Where there are big classes it can be difficult for school staffs to know an individual child intimately and many adults have commented on this lack in their later years. Family and individual initiative is most important and the broader the interests of the home the greater awareness your child can have about what line he or she wants to follow. An important book to buy or consult at your reference library is the careers guide published by the Central Youth Employment Executive (H.M.S.O.). This gives the fullest details of opportunities in the professions, industry and commerce with a description of the work, qualities of character and qualifications needed, training opportunities and prospects, financial and otherwise, and where to go for more detailed information. You will find such careers as Food Science and Technology, Dramatic Art, Dietetics, Plastics Technology, Dancing, Broadcasting (sound and television), Art and Design, Horticulture, the Merchant Navy, Hospital Management, Forestry, Laundry Management, Travel Agent, Town and Country Planning, and very many others. This is an extremely important source of reference, and job prospects are dealt with most realistically. Other useful books to know are *Middle School Choice* and *Upper School Choice*, published by the Careers Research and Advisory

Centre; *Which Career?* by Catherine Avent; and *Careers for Girls and Women*, published by the Women's Employment Federation. The Observer Student Service is geared to dealing with thousands of enquiries from young people wanting places on degree and diploma courses in polytechnics and other colleges outside the universities. Write to them at the Higher Education Advisory Centre, Enfield College (Middlesex Polytechnic), Queensway, Enfield, Middx, giving particulars of subjects studied, courses preferred and GCE qualifications (and sending a stamp for the reply).

When your child is earning you will have to decide how much he or she is to contribute to the home. What matters most here is that the contribution should be realistic. Where some widows may wish to put part of the weekly money into a special account for the child to use later on for wedding expenses or to set up house, others will need it all to meet overheads. If there have been family discussions on budgeting the children will not hesitate to contribute at least the student allowance of £7 per week. What helps most is to have a real understanding of the mother's needs, since she must go on fending for herself long after the children have left to make homes of their own.

Children are accustomed to having you to themselves and may have become most greedy of your services and of your time. You may have taken the easy course of pleading fatigue at the end of your day's work and stayed at home instead of creating new outside interests. Amongst children, the very young and those on the verge of leaving home are the ones who wish that their mothers would marry again. The success of a new marriage will depend on the capacity of the family to adapt, and sometimes older children genuinely wish to see their mothers looked after when they no longer need them themselves. A mother alone can be a real embarrassment to her older children, and this position may even be a source of much unhappiness if there is only one child. The dependent type of woman may cling to her adult child, seeking, in a state of panic, to keep him or her with her. If she remarries the hold on the children will inevitably loosen. There is a man to care for again.

Fathering another man's children is a job for a man who is fond of children anyway, and his success will be increased greatly if he loves their mother and the marriage is something more than one of convenience. He will then see the children not as embarrassing or hostile strangers but as part of his wife.

If you have remarried, you can't rush things in building the new family relationships. It all takes time, just as it did when you married first and when you had your children. There are no ready-made marriages. Inevitably you feel upset if the children and their stepfather are constantly at loggerheads. They must learn to live together too.

Many who handle difficult children recognize that, where the background is one of a fatherless home, the children in their delinquent acts are unconsciously calling for the return of the father and his secure authority. This does not mean that the stepfather must take up a policing role. His role will become easier as mutual understanding develops between him and the children. They will accept his authority better as they learn to like or love him and they will especially value him if he takes a protecting and caring part in any challenging relationship with the outer world of children or adults. The child with no 'Dad' feels a great loss of status amongst his fellows, even if he has more freedom for mischief.

Many of the widowed mothers who talk and write about remarriage lose sight of the fact that once grief is over they have a freedom of action which has some rewards. Those who use their time productively and, even if with some cost at first, go out into the world to work with, and to help, others may discover themselves in a new way. Abilities which have been submerged by the demands of a husband and growing family are discovered. I believe that where there is a second marriage and the new husband has a variety of hobbies and interests too, the pair may make a richer and more interesting relationship. Boredom with each other would be a fatal ingredient in developing the marriage, and the more interests suitable to the age groups of the partners the better. Here too is the need for the couple to think carefully in terms of common activity so that, with her new husband, the widow may weld the family together in its pleasures and enjoyments as well as in the ordinary discipline of the home.

This, however, is not a way that every widow can follow, and many do not remarry. For you there may be the launching of the children one after the other, and then a new life to be lived alone. This is when it takes a special courage to look outward to the world and inward to find your own potential.

The years of retirement bring decisions to be faced and new opportunities to be grasped too. Even if this time is still far in the future for you, you may have parents and in-laws who are about to retire. The Pre-Retirement Association offers membership and all sorts of positive ideas for enjoying retirement and for getting together to pursue interests. Their monthly magazine *Retirement Choice* comes as part of the subscription of £1·80 per annum, and members can contribute their own views to it.

10

Remarriage

Patterns of marriage determine type of
widowhood—The over-protected—Rigid attitudes of some men—All marriage a challenge
—Compensation in the Courts—Ageing men
and women—Marriage can be prostituted
—Idealizing the lost partner—Marrying again
with children—Other risks—Widows' views
—Can marriage bureaux help?

Many who have neither experienced widowhood in their own lives
nor seen it closely in the life of another woman have wondered
what all the fuss is about. Surely, they say, this is simply part of
living—people are born, people die. One must just rise above it.
Of course, life has other hazards too—physical, mental and material. What of them? Why should the widowhood of three million
women be significant in any way? In this chapter we are going to
look at marriage and at what remarriage offers, to see whether it
can help us to understand.

The pattern of marriage which lies behind the often devas-
tating experience of widowhood can sometimes be seen very
clearly. Those who have used the husband as a prop and leaned
heavily on him have a difficult time. It does not help a widow to
realize, too late, that she has been over-dependent in her marriage in order to build up her man's self-esteem; or that the
embellishment of the home, to the exclusion of community interests, has left her with nothing but things. Death has a painful
way of revealing true values.

Some women married 'from the schoolroom' develop in the
shadow of the husband, and often the widow does not know
who or what she really is. The exposure made by death can then
be both bewildering and heartbreaking. The deepest hurt is
found not necessarily where there was most love, but where
emotional security has been a haven and a crutch after an

unhappy childhood or youth. Such relationships, though very understandable, are only a half-way house to full personal development. Even those whose marriage is a ding-dong battle of wills may, as people, have achieved more maturity.

It may be true that the over-protective marriage is dying out, but there is ample evidence that many men still have a rigid and limiting attitude to women. Their own woman must not go out to work; she must not tire herself with voluntary activities or fill her mind with interests to rival his own. In a sense she is a 'belonging', a possession. For the wife to identify herself too closely with the world's struggles could well lead her to community service beyond the home. With a little subtle flattery some women may even fall for the temptation to extra ease and luxury in middle life, perhaps waking up too late to find husband and money gone, and few real bridges into the world outside.

Many books have been written dealing with the sexual patterns of marriage. These are varied and depend for their success on the partners' ability to satisfy each other's needs for loving. Where relationships and their physical demands have rhythm, sensitivity and expertise it would be unrealistic not to expect that a sense of great loss will follow the death of a partner. If the sex side of the marriage has been ill managed, has been built on fear, lust or lack of understanding of the natural female cycle, the male partner may still be mourned for other attributes he brought to the relationship.

There is no greater challenge than marriage with its intimacy and its changing climate of mood and circumstance. It will reveal a person's strength and weakness as nothing else will. Perhaps the best marriages are those where each of the partners grows bigger for the experience, becomes wholly a person, developing natural aptitudes and achieving satisfaction in work and life. For some widows this was so, and life together has been full of joy and richness. From such marriages a fruitful widowhood can come and because such women have given much they must go on doing so. They know no other way.

It would be unrealistic in such a book as this not to recognize the growing evidence of change in man/woman relationships. Already we can see these coming. Some are here in the attitude to sex and marital commitment seen in the lives of young people. The future is theirs and things will be different if they can make them so. Women are already making new demands of men, asking more of life than the lonely box-like existence of many marriages. They talk of group sex, of communes. In her book *The Future of Marriage* the sociologist Dr Jessie Barnard treats the subject with imagination and understanding. Writing about widowhood we must, of course, deal with what is; but we must be wideawake to change and its challenge.

I have said that well-meaning friends and relatives often tell the widow that she will marry again. Usually she will reject the idea at once, either as being a betrayal of her recent marriage partner or because the whole idea seems impossible. Nevertheless she feels flattered that she is still considered attractive enough for a second marriage. We are all too familiar with the court cases where widows are awarded lower compensation because the judge considers they are attractive propositions for remarriage. In all of this there is a subtle cruelty. Inevitably there are some women for whom life alone is utterly miserable and lonely. They are perhaps warm-hearted and good home-makers, but they are no longer young and the years have taken their toll, their capacity for stimulating the attention and interest of men is much reduced, and younger women may be exacting rivals. Of course we have all met the exceptions—women of vitality and interest who can bring unusual qualities to any relationship at any age. I am not, however, talking of them but of ordinary women who make up the partnership in average homes. What, in fact, is the truth of the matter? What can they reasonably expect? Of the three million widows in the British Isles, half a million are under fifty-four—the remainder are past middle age and must have unusual personal qualities or assets in kind if they are to hope for remarriage. There may be offers of marriage from the much older man who wants to be 'looked after' and for whom a widow may well have to face nursing, death and widowhood all over again; or from the widower with several children who is 'willing to offer marriage' if only to get a resident housekeeper to pull his home together. The new partner will then become stepmother, housekeeper and wife at one go. Without love, both she and he will need to be very special people to build anything good, or even lasting, out of this situation; indeed it will require selflessness on the part of both, a quality which is more likely to accompany the marriage which is commonly thought to have been 'made in heaven'. The middle-aged bachelor may await her too, probably now looking ruefully at his empty life and declining years and attractions. If selfishness and avoidance of responsibility are not the cause of his way of life and he is capable of loving, such a marriage might prove successful.

From the Abstract of Statistics we see that 0·56 per cent of widows in the United Kingdom remarried in 1971, that is six widows out of every thousand. The percentage is very slightly higher than in previous years, but so is the total number of widows. 2·1 per cent of widowers remarried in 1971.

With so large a population of widows it is better to look at the facts squarely and to view the chances of those who really wish to remarry in their light. Most widows will probably lead a happier life and have a clearer determination to make something of it, if they dismiss remarriage as something of a dream. Accepting this, it nevertheless remains part of the purpose of this book to consider all the aspects of renewal a widow may wish for or find.

Those in the younger group may have many advances made to them, though not all with marriage in mind. Young marriages which have been happy usually contain a strong romantic element, and where this is so it may be very hard to accept a new mate. Memory of the marriage and the freshness of it all are still there—the children perhaps are still tiny and dependent. Should the young widow be one of a social group of contemporaries she may be sought in marriage by someone younger than herself who has not yet assayed marriage and finds her attractive because of her experience of it. She may be approached by an older man who for various reasons is still hesitating to take the plunge, by a man whose marriage is broken or by a much older protective 'father figure', probably a widower. If the young widow can hold her own for a time and also find inner healing, she will be able to make a new start with a second family to follow. Romantic comparisons may be difficult because she has not the longer experience of companionship and sharing that the older widow treasures. Depending on her maturity she may be able to make a successful union with a single man, but she will have to be sure that he fully accepts her husband's children too, and that his unmarried state, if he is older than she, is not the outward evidence of immaturity, mother fixation or selfishness. Such a man is hardly likely to make a good father or stepfather. The younger she is the less likely she is to have the tolerance and forgiveness such a marriage could demand. If she chooses a man with a broken marriage she will need to understand the reasons for the breakdown, and there may be one or two children to add to her own too. The addition of further children in these circumstances would put the full test on the new partnership. Finally, she may be persuaded to take the perhaps temporary comfort and security offered by the much older 'father figure'. This has its very clear risks and an on-going price for both partners which should be faced. She may soon find that she is no longer in step with her contemporaries and may encounter a new loneliness. Her older husband will need special qualities of adaptability to accept her younger men and women friends. To be forewarned here may even be especially helpful to the younger wife. She should strive to keep her own friends. So even the young widow has special problems to face, although we know one in five does find a second mate.

If the older woman with a longer marriage behind her feels that a good chapter in life, and not a bad one, has ended, a new marriage, if it is to have any success, must be seen as just that, and not a copy of something that went before. As each of us responds differently to different people so the earlier marriage can never be repeated. The widow is different herself too, and her second husband is quite another person. Everything is new, but that does not mean that the clock is turned back to young romance. The love of older people is likely to be a deeper and more tried emotion, and if they have both been married, and have not waited too long, they may be both adaptable and understanding.

If remarriage plans are based only on material objectives they carry their own risks. The partners must then be prepared to accept far less than in their first marriage and build the new relationship on a different basis. In the intimacy of marriage this can be exceedingly difficult if not impossible. While we know that love in both men and women can go on to the end of the normal life span, a man who marries a woman without this, but for the service she can give the home, risks her sexual withdrawal very soon. Everything may depend on initial attraction, maintained attractiveness in both partners in the face of age, and the capacity of the man to understand and woo his woman.

Of course there are women so desperately in need of reassurance, or so lonely, that they will take any relationship that is offered. Here the partners simply make use of each other. It is rarely the basis of real loving nor is it likely to become so. Perhaps the majority of women are fortunate in that their natural tendency is to look for relationship before they look for sex.

In their book, *Sex in Marriage*, Baruch and Miller comment helpfully on remarriage: 'Realistically, a husband or wife can replace another only with his or her own individual abilities, with his or her own unique personality, with skills, with shortcomings, with moods—which in their totality make this person different from anyone else. One person cannot detract from another particular person's place in our hearts; this new husband or wife is new. We two make a new combination, not a duplication. And so we ourselves become new people in a sense. Different parts of us are drawn out, different parts of us are taxed. Different parts of us find enjoyment. Different parts of us must learn to tolerate strain. And, if our abilities have changed, have not stultified, we will find in all of this a challenge to adapt and fit in our own ways of life so as to make a new creative design.

'After a partner's death there is sometimes a tendency to idealize the lost marriage. Then a new marriage cannot have its proper chance to bring its own satisfaction and no living marriage of flesh and blood and two people's personalities can possibly be as perfect as the idyllic memory, shorn of the struggle that every human relationship holds. When the marriage that was interrupted by death was not too happy the unhappiness may be obscured or forgotten because of the death. The world may look upon the widow or widower as a better marriage risk than the divorced man or woman. But the person himself, if he is honest, may have just as many doubts about himself:

'"To tell the truth, I was no better a husband to my first wife, who died, than I was to my second, who got a divorce. I made the same mistakes. The first wife took it: the second didn't. And as for me, I could hide them from myself and the world the first time, since death has no tongue, but the last time I couldn't. So, since I want this next time to be better, I had better change some things in myself."

'Although each new marriage is a new adventure, a former marriage invariably leaves its imprint. However, deeper imprints are left from far earlier. For any marriage actually starts at birth. And so, if we want to discover what will help us to live this new chance creatively, then we must go back to the very things we needed to consider in relation to the original marriage; the very things that make sex function freely or that make marriage and "the good life" go hand in hand. We will want to understand, for instance, that all of us marry to gain some profoundly and universally desired satisfaction; but into every marriage each person also brings his own individual wants and needs. Every normal marriage has its problems, and love and sharing and sex and sharing go hand in hand. Each of us holds deeply within us the longing to be understood and both of us therefore need to develop the art of understanding and the courage to confide.'

In Chapter 9 I have mentioned some of the difficulties which may either make remarriage impossible or spoil it when there are children. It is enough to say here that not only must the children accept the mother's new husband, but care has to be taken to make a fair and equitable arrangement for them in all matters before the marriage takes place. Unhappily the widow's allowance for the children ceases when she remarries, and this can become a source of trouble. The family allowance makes too small a contribution to be significant. This is especially important where the children are already of knowledgeable and sensible years. Depending on their age, a mother may decide to give them any inheritance from their natural father before remarrying. If an adoption decision is made by the new husband this cannot usually be effected until some months after the second marriage.

In a group discussion of widows the subject of remarriage can be treated very candidly. It was interesting to note on one such occasion that advice recommended for others was not necessarily what the widows accepted for themselves. On the whole they felt the idea of remarriage was excellent if there were no children or if they were grown up. There did not appear to be great confidence in the average man's love of other men's children, and there were other problems.

'I couldn't go through those years of nursing again,' said one. 'I couldn't face the re-adapting after six years managing alone,' said another. 'It would never be the same and I'd be afraid of being disappointed.' 'I've discovered myself in a new way since my husband died; before then I was always considering him. I can't give up my new life now. I feel I'm somebody in my own right at last.' 'I should be embarrassed before the children—sharing a bed and all that. . . .' 'How do I know he would like, let alone love, my children?' 'Whose side would I take if they ran across each other? I should feel torn between them.' 'Oh, that wouldn't worry me. I'd take the first chance of remarriage that offered and the children could lump it.' 'What would you do about your relatives—your first husband's relatives too? Wouldn't you have to cut them out? It all seems too complicated to be worth it.' 'I think when you're young everything seems romantic somehow—you'll tackle anything—take it in your stride. When you're older and have been through the mill, you haven't the same blindness. You see the pitfalls.' 'I want a man in my home to control my boys. I'm sick of the battles.' 'My children don't want to share me—they've got me all to themselves.' 'What happens when your children leave home? You're properly alone then, aren't you?' 'Yes, and you definitely aren't young any more.'

Puzzled uncertainties seem to prevail. Someone summed it up: 'Of course, what we really want is our own man back, the one we chose and married when we were young. We grew together in marriage, laughed at each other's weaknesses, shared memories, happy and sad.' 'I think one loses one's capacity to adapt to living intimately with another person if one is alone too long. One should remarry in the second year, before one is too set.' 'That may be, but how do you meet in our sort of social set-up?'

In Peter Marris's book, *Widows and their Families*, he notes that most of the widows in his inquiry met their second husband through friends and relatives, at work, dancing and, in one instance, at the cemetery. The fear of failure seems, in Marris's investigation, to haunt these marriages in proportion to the happiness of the first marriage. I quote his words:

'In general, therefore, it seems likely that the second marriage of widows will be under a greater strain than the first. If the marriage is contracted for mutual convenience, husband and wife have only tolerance and gratitude to withstand the irritations that grow with familiarity. A man who marries a widow for love needs uncommon tact and humility, since he must share her affection with a now unimpeachable rival, whose loss she still mourns . . . the step relationships further complicate the conflict of loyalties.' Marris found that the contentment of the marriage on the widow's part was measured by the little she expected of it.

Perhaps women are too unrealistic in hoping for a second

romance, especially when so much importance is laid on physical appearance in both sexes and the stress of present-day life has taken its toll in health and the ageing process. Already the changing status of women and the proportion of numbers in the sexes are encouraging more exacting demands by women where men are concerned. The tradition women follow in attention to their appearance, and the fact that they have a longer expectation of life than men, may change the age patterns in marriage too. To reach the end of life together in marriage seems reasonable.

The figures for remarriage already quoted indicate how few widows can hope to remarry in later life. It is therefore not surprising that those who desperately seek another mate as the solution to all their ills will turn to the possibility of using a marriage bureau. One thing is abundantly clear: the need has called these agencies into existence and, judging by the rapid growth of this service for lonely people, we can guess that marriage bureaux are here to stay. It is, all the same, most important to be completely aware of the limitations in this special approach to marriage. It has been estimated that about 5,000 marriages a year actually come about through the various bureaux in Britain—not, we must admit, a very large number. Estimates indicate that six bureaux alone have 16,000 clients on their registers and that the total number of bureaux in this country may be well in the region of 1,000.

From the widow's point of view the remarriage figures are particularly disappointing, as they hold out little hope for her. Some bureaux refuse to take on the older woman, knowing they can do little for her, others have fewer scruples. We can, of course, leave a special place for the older widow with means which she is prepared to set down on the altar of remarriage through a bureau. She must indeed be a hard-headed business woman—and more —to pull off such a deal satisfactorily. In working-class spheres, where investigations are rough and ready, a man and woman may take a chance on setting up home, and either or both partners may produce family complications after the wedding day. 'He never told me his son was in Borstal, so it evens up with my defective daughter he didn't know about who is away in a school.' This can be a dangerous game to play.

According to investigations churchgoers and non-churchgoers use marriage bureaux equally. Only one bureau in England claims to be specifically Christian. It charges five to fifteen guineas if a marriage results, which sum must be paid before the wedding. A Catholic bureau charges only one guinea registration and three or four guineas for the first introduction. In any difficulty the priest's help is called in. An Irish bureau, run by a trained social worker, charges no fees. Applicants must give a clergyman's and a doctor's reference. One bureau takes fees from anyone between eighteen and eighty. The bureau claiming greatest marriage successes accepts only a limited number of women over thirty-five. Those who register are a social cross-section. As persons, many are lonely retiring folk who cannot make their own relationships easily. The majority of men enrolled are over fifty and widowers, but some bureaux carry a considerable number of divorcees. In all cases introductory meetings are arranged, when the two parties go out together, probably meeting over a meal. To many women the reality of the situation is more than they can contemplate, even if they have got past the interview at the bureau, when their 'assets' are examined. As far as I have been able to discover the total financial commitments can vary from nothing to £100. The arrangements carry no guarantee that a woman will not involve herself with a bigamist, a psychopath, a sexual pervert or a ne'er-do-well. She must accept this risk. It has also frequently been noted that, of the men and women who apply to register at marriage bureaux, the women tend to be the more satisfactory of the two sexes. This is undoubtedly because the male in our community usually prefers to hunt his mate himself, whereas the woman is in the difficult position of having to declare herself as available for marriage. In this country it has not yet been found possible to apply controls which would safeguard those who register. This has been attempted in Holland, where there are a number of non-profit-making bureaux with quite considerable statutory controls. They keep in close touch with one another and are supervised by a committee of parsons, doctors and psychiatrists with other married people to assist them in interviewing. It is significant that after initial screening 20 per cent of the unmarried men are rejected where only 5 per cent of the women are turned away. The success rate is said to be 25 per cent for women and 60 per cent for men—a reflection of the proportion of women and men who apply.

Reviewing the marriage bureau method as it is operated in

Britain I am inclined to think that a Samaritan priest I once met in Israel, who was also a marriage broker, might be more successful. For him every aspect of the family histories of the would-be partners in a marriage had to be laid bare and failures on his part could certainly haunt him. Far greater controls are desirable if those who register with most marriage bureaux in Britain are to be protected fully. Failing this only the widow with a sharp knowledge of the world and some protection in it is wise to use this method of finding a second mate.

Undoubtedly some will feel that to go to a marriage bureau would seem like taking a stand at the last ditch and that it is better to cut your losses and face life with realism. Being alone is part of it, although loneliness need not be. To learn to love yourself and your neighbour is an expansion in living, and both are essential if there is to be any contentment in widowhood. It is after all a life which demands a special kind of maturity, embodying as it does that pattern of joy and pain which most of us experience.

Without doubt man/woman relationships are undergoing considerable change and something of the new pattern may well become clear before our children reach middle age. What can be seen already is the lop-sided development of men and women as individuals, where rigid role-playing cripples the sensitive man and the creative woman. As Laurens van der Post has said, men must learn to know and live with the feminine in themselves and women must accept greater responsibilities and come out of married seclusion. Through the years each sex has been 'hobbled' by society and the liberation of both men and women could mean very significant changes in the lot of widowers and, even more so, of widows. In a sense each sex needs to know the marriage of the opposites in themselves before entering into commitment to each other. Such an approach will mean far less crippling in widowhood, which could then become an experience with its own rewards.*

* See Addenda, page 185.

11

Life is what you are alive to

A new look at your health to start with—The
menopause can be a worry—Sexual deprivation
and what doctors say—Ideas on activity and
exercise—Disability—Living with neighbours—Lack of money need not cramp you
—Life enrichment—Make your brain work for
you—Various ideas—Using libraries—Meeting
and making men friends—Women's clubs
—Helping other people—A different type of
holiday—Emigrating.

What, you probably want to know, *is* a full life for a widow? Is it
possible even in early or late middle years to create for yourself a
new and satisfying way of living? As a married woman you may
have thought you had this, but now you realize it was a life for
two, or for a family, and it was built in that pattern, to a large
degree centred on a man. What you have now is quite different.
Even with the companionship of your children you still know you
are alone. To deal with any form of rebuilding, to begin again, is
far from easy, but it can be done, and I am going to talk about it in
this chapter.

First of all I suggest starting with your general health. If you do
not learn to look after yourself from now on no one else will! Obviously you must have medical advice if you are nervous and jit-
tery and constantly worried. If you can't sleep, have headaches,
get attacks of breathlessness, are always tired, lose weight, have
skin trouble, heavy periods, rheumatism (these are all symptoms
widows complain about), you should talk them over with your
doctor. The confidence you have in him or her will be a great support at this time. Some widows say it is easier to talk to a woman.
You will be the first to realize that it is no good talking about new
beginnings if your physical condition is poor, so first and fore-
most deal with health worries and see that you get on top of them.

Have a combined cervical and breast check and see your dentist too. This is a time when many widows neglect themselves and your health is now one of your most important assets.

So many widows lose their men during the menopause years that we ought to give this often disturbing phase in every woman's life some attention. This is more important as its discomfort must be faced alone. You can't rely on your doctor having time to explain things to you unless you're especially fortunate, or have a sympathetic woman doctor who knows first-hand what it means. The menopause, climacteric or 'change of life' is the phase of changeover in the female mechanism which produces an egg every month. The glands which maintain this elaborate childbearing system work as a team for over thirty years. If the change comes about slowly some glands take over from those going out of action and the system settles quietly, perhaps hardly noticeably. If, however, the glandular substance called oestrogen, which is manufactured each month, suddenly diminishes as it does in some women, discomfort follows. During this time of glandular imbalance, when the whole personality can be disturbed, some women are helped by being given small doses of oestrogen so that the process becomes more gradual. The time of discomfort may vary from eighteen months to several years. The commonest age for the end of periods is fifty, but they may be intermittent or altered in cycle for some time before then. Undue frequency or flooding in periods should be watched, as this may lead to anaemia. Shock may stop menstruation suddenly too, as some widows have found to their dismay. For up to two years after the normal end of the periods a woman can still become pregnant and she is ill-advised to forget this. Where menstruation is brought to an end by the operation to remove the ovaries, menopausal symptoms may still follow.

The positive thing about all this is that women often have a new lease of life after the menopause, and can indeed expect it. Hot flushes are a symptom most are glad to see the last of. These are due largely to oestrogen deficiency and vary in intensity from wet sweating to an all-over feeling of warmth. Sedatives are often prescribed. It may interest women tempted to feel sorry for themselves to know that middle-aged men can experience the same symptom. Other physical and psychological responses to this changeover period can include moods of irritability and depression. We are told that what is a usual part of a woman's personality, even if normally well controlled, will be more evident at this time. It could be laziness, cussedness, a fighting spirit or even a tendency to feel persecuted or martyred. Other physical symptoms may include migraine, dizziness, the racing heart sensation, rheumatism, skin trouble, growth of superfluous hair and shrinkage of the vaginal passage. It is improbable, fortunately, that any woman will suffer more than one or two of these troubles, but if they bother her she should discuss aids with her doctor. It is possibly not without significance that many of the symptoms experienced in the menopause are similar to those noted in the first year or two of widowhood. Many women feel the end of the fertility period as a real deprivation or bereavement. Its advantages, however, soon become apparent. We know, for example, that there is often increased mental energy when women are over the menopause. Some discover unsuspected gifts of artistic creativity and new cultural interests. There is a new bodily freedom. In Chapter 6 I discuss matters relating to your personal appearance. They are even more important now when you face your world alone.

For most women to find themselves alone and without masculine companionship when they have lived in partnership is a profound and disturbing loss. It might seem that without this closeness and cherishing life becomes dull and heavy. If you are worried about sexual deprivation, don't be. It will do you no harm, although you may find it hard to bear when the time of shock and tiredness leaves you. Dr Isadore Ruben in his most helpful book has the following realistic comments to make on sexual deprivation in widowhood: 'A strategy for living must take into account those who are widowed and have no other opportunity for sexual release than masturbation.' He quotes a pioneering counselling psychologist and marriage consultant who recommends that this release should be accepted as a perfectly valid outlet when there is a need and other means of gratification are not available. He speaks of a widow who consulted him because she was worried about the self-stimulation she had practised since her husband's death five years before. This had been within the pattern of her married sex life and she had thought that, if it was wrong, he might give her medicine to stop it. The doctor advised her to accept auto-erotic relief as a perfectly proper outlet and not to worry about it. Dr Laura Hutton, formerly of the Tavistock Clinic, has said: 'Research has in fact shown that women who have practised self-stimulation for years have had a better health record than those who under pressure of a sense of guilt have given up the habit.' She recommends women in this situation to get it over and forget about it, turning to their work with increased energy and ease of mind. 'The whole thing is unimportant and concerns yourself alone.' It is probably also wise for women to do daily interior muscle exercise to keep the vaginal muscles strong.

This then is the moment when, in her new life, a widow takes stock of her health. The shock of bereavement leaves its mark, often in considerable fatigue: but this is temporary and the time will come when you feel alive again and new relationships and new interests can take over. Two years is a reasonable time for physical and mental readjustment. You may or may not remarry, but it is very probable that you have more than twenty years of active life ahead. So health and exercise matter. Do not rely on household chores and gardening to keep you fit. The basis of your new life may call for quite a new regime if you are to make something good of it. First of all your weight should be checked and diet reviewed. After thirty-five care needs to be taken over increased weight and unnecessary bulges. Both can be attacked with sensible eating, exercise and appropriate activities.

A regular ten minutes of deep breathing and rhythmic movement with extension stretching, followed by five minutes of total quiet and relaxation, will be a better lead into your day than a fevered anxious rush. Most people rarely fill their lungs and expel the air fully. This should be done daily with the air reasonably warm. Exercises too should be done with the body warm so that muscles respond easily. Cycling may be an ideal form of movement for a lot of women, taking weight off the feet and using all the tummy muscles. Those who want the exercise without the machine, and the added advantage of head standing, can 'cycle' in the air supporting the hips from the waist. For women who are constrained and anxious, relaxed free dancing will do them more good than physical jerks. All you need is to push back the furniture in a convenient room and shut the door on the family! Many have joined Health and Beauty, Music and Movement or Yoga classes and felt a new sense of wellbeing. These classes are often filled with middle-aged and older women who have overcome unnecessary self-consciousness. Clothing is no problem as most wear jump suits, tights or shorts and blouses. For neatness black or navy is probably the best colour for the job.

Another form of exercise which can be taken, alone or with a friend, is swimming. This uses all the body muscles, takes weight off the feet and gives the delight of being in another element. Skating—which after all does not require a partner—can be very releasing and tremendous fun. Both golf and archery can be practised alone and lead to competition and new relationships. Remember by the way that golf, bowls and swimming can be taken up when you are over fifty. If acceptance in a women's bowling team is possible, this gives much enjoyment, whereas younger women might prefer to team up for ten-pin bowling in the evenings. Those who can afford it may return to riding, but this can be lonely and costly. Dancing, whether folk, Scottish or ballroom, is most enjoyable, and if there is a Cruse Club active locally it is easier to form a small party. Many town halls run regular dances which are most happy occasions where older people and women can go together. Caledonian Societies cater for Scottish dancing, and the English Folk Dance and Song Society have a full and fascinating programme. Usually local institutes will teach folk dancing if there are enough people wishing to learn. If you like walking you can return to this enjoyable activity on week-end outings in the company of the Ramblers' Association, or the Youth Hostels Association which welcomes people of all ages. Parties go regularly to well-known walking areas, and a day spent this way is both marvellously healthy and rewarding in fellowship. If you live within reach of London the London Appreciation Society has a friendly membership and groups go together to discover with expert guides new interests in the city. One thing is certain: you will have in one way or another to break new ground in your physical activity if you want to enjoy life. It is quite useless to remain at home waiting to be taken out! You will simply stagnate mentally and physically.

If you have any form of physical disability you will be wise to enrol with the organization having your special interests at heart. A go-ahead organization started by two disabled women, and called the Disablement Income Group, is also well worth joining.

Most women are interested in the creative side of life and this is often the core of much of their inner satisfaction. When children begin to be independent the moment comes for you to strike out to new interests. It is better too if this is done while your children are still at home. To wait until the house is empty may be to find courage in short supply. And courage it does need to move out from the shelter of the home to take part in community affairs and a working life.

Your relationship with your neighbours is an important part of your new life as a widow. To live in harmony with them will make a lot of difference and to know you can call on them at a time of need is a source of strength. If you too will give your help when you see it is needed without having to be asked you will be warmly welcomed. If you have a busy mother next door, and have time yourself, give help of a practical nature. When your neighbour is lonely help her by being a good listener. Your time for talking will come later. Whatever you do try to take the goodwill of your neighbours for granted.

As a widowed mother, or a widow alone, obviously some activities will be beyond your means, and you may feel that lack of money halts you at every turn. You may even feel that any creative pursuit must have a financial return to be worth your time. But whichever way you look at it, there is a void now that must be filled. This search for life enrichment has many sides. You may, for example, want to know more about philosophy, religion and psychology. If you already have religious affiliations this could be the time to extend your interest and to attend special meetings on your Church's programme to study the teaching at a deeper level. Help with children's work or youth clubs in the Church or joining a branch of the Church's 'Fish' scheme for neighbourly help may appeal to you. If you feel drawn to some different form of worship but have no Church, you may want to explore other approaches, including the more formal, decorative and musical or the more simple and austere. I offer a few suggestions in the Appendix. You may be happier with special societies and their teaching, or prefer to look to some of the exponents of age-old spiritual teachings. Interesting lectures to attend are often advertised in the appropriate column of the national press or in weekly journals such as the *New Statesman*. What really matters for those who feel a sense of desperate loneliness and inner poverty is that they should find their roots and deepen their awareness of spiritual forces which are universal and timeless. To ask questions of oneself and of others is often to fling open doors.

If you want to increase your understanding of yourself and other people you will find suitable courses in elementary psychology at most evening institutes. Here the exchange of ideas in the class can be most rewarding and you will meet like-minded people. There is a brief list of helpful books on personal relationships in the Appendix. The 'Friendship through Study' groups run by the National Adult School Union offer an opportunity for people of differing backgrounds to share ideas and interests. Informal discussions on all aspects of society are a good way of making friends, and local groups can be started with the help of the N.A.S.U. Women who join any evening class course on international or local government affairs will develop a wholly new interest and meet men and women of broader outlook too. Those with political interests will now find they have time to work with their local party headquarters.

There are many subjects which can open quite new fields of interest and relationship with people: languages, literature, theatre, poetry, ballet, architecture, history, astronomy and current affairs are only a few of them. What matters is that the chosen subject should be given full attention and, where possible, linked to spare-time reading, to holiday courses and contacts with others. Those who have followed such a plan have not only made new friends but found more to share and to discuss, themselves becoming more interesting people to others and more aware of the world round them. Each special subject studied nearly always leads to something else. If you take up a language you will find new interest in travel, companions to go with and new friends among foreign visitors. You may become a hostess to lonely foreigners and, before you know where you are, yourself be teaching them English! There is hardly a small town without its quota of foreigners needing help in mastering our language and in dealing with their loneliness.

If you live in the Greater London area a worth-while activity is to become a voluntary tutor under the Cambridge House Literacy Scheme for adult illiterates. Since all pupils are over school age, tuition usually has to be given in the evening or at weekends; the pupil may come to you, but if you travel to him, or her, the pupil is expected to pay your expenses. This work has its social side too, as tutors train together in small groups and keep in touch through meetings and correspondence. The enterprising among you might offer to help those with reading and writing problems in your own area.

If you love poetry and literature you may begin or join a writers' or readers' circle. The history, archaeology or architecture enthusiast can join the Historical Association, county societies and make excursions with others to study churches, old buildings and sites and perhaps join 'digs' with an archaeology team. In this connection there is often indoor work too.

Those who are nature lovers may prefer bird watching, field studies or weather study at an Air Ministry reporting station.

A fascinating activity we can often see in an old church is brass rubbing. This may be a family occupation with the children and include cycle rides or rambling expeditions. It is, by the way, courtesy to ask permission from the vicar and to offer a gift to the church. Although time must be allowed to do the job, it combines cheapness with the achievement of a wall decoration which can be the envy of many and may have some sale value. A hobby which can be shared with young people is stamp collecting and, given time, the collection can even be worth something! Of course there are endless amusing and interesting subjects for collection; the more original the better, and they need not be expensive. You will have your own ideas. You will find the books on collecting and restoring junk, by John Bedford, most stimulating, but try to pursue your searches and the outcome with a friend or group. 'You've broken it, I'll mend it', could be your slogan for tackling all sorts of small repairs for friends and neighbours, using the wide selection of adhesives now available. You might even build up quite a little business! The book *Mending China* will help here. Amongst the art pursuits, painting, drawing, clay modelling, pottery and weaving all have their place. Most can be learned in evening or institute classes. A natural aptitude is a help, but many have had great enjoyment from no great achievement, while others can discover an ability they never knew they had. One experience is common to all who take up these arts: they will become wholly absorbed in them.

Some women have a longing to follow more masculine pursuits and, with no man about to rival them, they readily take to carpentry and car maintenance. Here again there are nearly always local classes to be found, usually with some women in them!

If you have always wanted to give time to music you can either build on earlier teaching or start for the first time. Any music which is performed in a group is better for people who are lonely, and some types of instrument, such as the guitar (learned in a few weeks, they say!) or accordion, may have an additional appeal for the younger folk in your family. The recorder creates a link with folk song and dance and is easy to learn. The special pleasure of choral or choir singing is well attested and certainly many choirs have vacancies. If you write to the local choirmaster he may call you up to see him to hear your voice. It is not always necessary to be a regular member of a church where you offer to help in the choir.

Another enjoyable group activity is bell ringing.

Many who read this book will themselves have interesting ideas for spare-time activity. We cannot know it all! What matters is to find the place to learn and to meet others. In the local setting usually the best plan is to visit the library and study the social activities list. This may also be found at the Citizens' Advice Bureau. A visit to the library will remind you too what pleasant places these can be, not only in providing a fine selection of books but very often in giving comfort and quiet in which to read. The reference library always has the daily papers and weekly magazines and periodicals. A regular browse for those with time is the most fruitful occupation. If you are following a special study course you can also ask for books to be sent from other libraries. The great thing about a library is to learn to use it well.

Man is by nature a gregarious animal, and woman certainly is too. Even 'keeping oneself to oneself' in the marriage relationship as some do is better than living like a hermit, but however limited your social life may have been in your marriage you may well find that this ends with the loss of your partner. To have suddenly to break new ground in meeting others is not easy, but it must be done if your new life is to have meaning and richness. Hobbies and common interests are great uniters, but the simple business of getting together to talk is important too. Women who have been married are used to men, their thinking and ways, and often they demand mixed clubs and are most disappointed to find few or none. Where attempts have been made to start such clubs men are much outnumbered and few enjoy being in a social situation where they are in the minority. Men, it seems, go to pubs to chat and to clubs to share common interests. The woman going on her own to a pub is still somewhat rare and, unless she shares male interests, she will not easily find male companionship. Many widows find they are no longer invited to mixed gatherings and a lot of doors are now closed to them. On very special occasions to have a male escort may be most essential, but this costs money. The Eros Escort and Guide Service in London has men of impeccable background on its list who escort a woman for any function or outing.

In political clubs and in churches you will find men, usually with their wives. The widower or the somewhat rare bachelor will, for the most part, already have chosen activities, wife-hunting probably not among them. If you are a very young widow you have your family to tie you down, and must make special plans if you are to be free. Not unnaturally you will want to meet men, and how to do this will often be a problem. Some towns have regular dances you can go to with a woman friend, but apart from this you must rely on the community centre, sports clubs and special activity groups. Some towns have Solo Clubs for lonely people. The Citizens' Advice Bureau will give you details.

Perhaps here it is appropriate to talk about friendships with men. These may seem few and far between, but you can be sure they will crop up in different forms, some of them unhappily not at all what you had expected or were used to. The sheer loneliness of some widows, and their lack of actual physical protection, can leave them open to approaches they are surprised and even dismayed to receive. In the nature of things the majority of the men will be married with wives and families of their own. While a temporary affair may boost some women's morale, it may also set tongues wagging and cast you as a 'merry widow' available for 'fun' and to be avoided by 'nice' people. You very soon find that, even in what are called 'enlightened days', 'it's the man who gets the pleasure—the woman who gets the pain'. On the other hand, perhaps, women are not the losers if they reject the philandering role.

The difficulty for most married women is that they have long since chosen real relationship as preferable to the casual variety, even though many of their daughters are trying the man's way of freedom with 'the pill' as their safeguard. This way, however, can mean for a widow a painful emotional involvement in which she is free and the man friend is not. Of the two of you it is probable that you will be the more hurt because you are not in your nature a trifler, but basically a loving, caring person who, through no fault of yours, has an empty home and heart. The man's need for extra-marital relationship may be no more than greed, and when the crunch comes he will stand by his wife and home. At best the alternative is that he will turn to you and hope for a divorce from his wife which she may not be willing to give.

Heather Jenner speaks with frankness on this subject: 'Because a woman has to take the responsibilities for her own actions entirely on her own shoulders, she thinks about them, and this is likely to make her more moral in the true sense of the word rather than less. The stigma of "naughtiness" is going. It is difficult for a woman to be naughty if everybody is simply expecting her to make her own decisions, and she is more likely to be thought weak-minded than anything else if she persistently makes wrong decisions and rushes from one man to another. The same applies to men. If a man has affairs with quantities of women, public opinion nowadays is more likely to decide that there is something wrong with him than that he is particularly glamorous. . . . The older a woman gets the more complicated sex relationship becomes, as it does if she has been married before. I think that whatever she decides, a woman is very stupid to live openly with a man. If she has an affair with him she should make it quite clear that officially they have their own establishments . . . it is the woman's reputation that suffers more than the man's even in these emancipated days. If she lives openly in the man's home she is in a subservient position, and if he lives in hers she is criticized for not even being able to find a man with a home of his own. If the relationship does not lead to a real one the man still comes off best, however broad-minded she and her friends may be. A woman loses more than a man does through being unconventional.' (From *The Marriage Book*.)

If you are young and attractive and have children you will have to be doubly careful, as jealous tongues may get busy. 'My neighbour's wife would sooner burn the potatoes than leave him talking to me over the fence.' 'I got so fed up with workmen's attitudes when they had a job in my house, I just went out for the day to avoid them.' 'I had so many unexpected advances from husbands of friends I started to keep clear of them all. I didn't want any of them. They didn't seem to realize I was still grieving for my husband.' Somehow this is all very far from a loving relationship and smacks more of being 'used' than of mutual respect and genuine care. But you may find some men who seek your company because 'you are you', although opening your home to them will always have its social problems. Some will be widowers, starved like you of the comfort of a shared home. You may enjoy their company occasionally with no wish for more. You can at least talk the common language of married life and practical cares. Much too will depend on whether you have lived an 'open house' pattern in your marriage, and whether you are quite clear in your own mind about what you want and what you do not want. Havelock Ellis has said with some truth: 'Trust and sexual rightness is not easily achieved outside the marriage bed.' While we can see considerable evidence of change in the patterns of sexual relationships, for many widows long sheltered in marriage this is often true.

To commit themselves in close relationship may mean an emotional 'pair bonding' on one side only, with much hurt for one partner if it is broken. In time we shall see changes in the woman's role and one day there may even be a copy in our society of the present-day Japanese social club where women alone can find temporary male partners. One practical point which it is well to remember is that if you cohabit with a man in your house your pension is forfeited. It follows that some discretion is necessary where a widow has a male lodger. There will always be those ready to say, with or without truth, that he shares your bed.

Although the following groups contain a proportion of widows, the main centres of social life for married women with their men at home are undoubtedly the Women's Institute, the Townswomen's Guild, the Mothers' Union, Toc H Women's Group and the Y.W.C.A. Others relate more particularly to husband's work, services' life, political or professional interests or hobbies. Unhappily many widows can feel very cut off from their erstwhile friends who still have their married lives and activities. There may be outings, subscriptions and appeals which the widow can no longer afford. For this reason some, not unnaturally, prefer an organization of their own where their situation and difficulties are understood and accepted. With such support many have felt better able to face the married community of women and have been able to contribute more effectively. Nevertheless it is wise to maintain a firm relationship with the married community. Cruse has always sought to encourage this rather than to create a separatist group of widows alone.

So although in many ways as a widow you may find you have to work harder, and your time can be more taken up, nevertheless there are many hours when you feel very much alone. Much depends on work and home ties. In choosing what club or group you want to join you may decide too in what field you would like to give help: to the old, the young, the sick, the disabled, the blind, the mentally ill, to the Church, to the pursuit of peace, to politics or to education. Most of these require help of all kinds and you will make friends giving it. Again some modicum of persistence is needed in finding out what is available locally. Usually the Citizens' Advice Bureau can help here. I give names of the main organizations to which to apply for more details with addresses in the Appendix. The National Association of Women's Clubs also carries full details regarding local clubs for women in many parts of the country.

Those who consider doing voluntary social work may wish to consult the Social Work Advisory Service or the National Council of Social Service, who produce a detailed list of different kinds of social service opportunity.

Probably the best way to consider the approach to any form of community service you may wish to do is to classify it under disablement and general community needs. Here are some ideas:

The Disabled　The blind, deaf, arthritic, paralysed, limbless, mentally subnormal, cancer patients, the mentally sick, drug takers, alcoholics, people in hospital.

Children　Orphans, spastics, autistic and disturbed children.

Social Problems　Problem families, prisoners (and their families), the old and infirm, unmarried mothers, separated and divorced, immigrants, refugees and family emergencies of all kinds.

General Community Activities　The following may badly need

your practical help: Friends of local hospitals, Youth Clubs, Coffee Clubs, International Friendship groups, Parent Teacher associations, Workers' Educational Association, Adult Education, Parents' National Education Union, Girl Guides, Brownies, Cubs, Y.W.C.A., Family Planning, Marriage Guidance, 'Fish' schemes, School Care Service, Women's Royal Voluntary Service, Family Service Units, Citizens' Advice Bureau, Old People's Welfare.

This list is by no means comprehensive but it is a beginning. If you have never done public work you will want to gain experience. You may be especially fitted for some of the organizations requiring particular knowledge. What matters is that you find your right niche and give reliable and regular help. It is a fact of experience that you yourself will gain immeasurably and very often quite out of proportion to what you give. Of this you may rest assured: you really are needed.

There is no doubt that holidays take on a new look in your widowhood. They can be the high light of your year, to plan and to save for, and to look forward to. They can be taken with a friend, alone or with the children. Experience shows that many widows are at first very shy about going alone, and if they try to repeat the same kind of hotel holiday they had with their husbands it is often a miserable failure. Accepting that a change and rest from routine are exceptionally important for someone who is carrying all her problems alone, it is wise to take a holiday with a new approach. If the children are still too young to go away alone, it is probably the happiest solution to keep them with you, and avoid the feelings of insecurity which can follow your seeming desertion of them if you go away without them. You can probably more easily manage a week-end house party on your own later on, leaving the children at home with a relative in charge.

So if it's to be a family holiday, a house-party atmosphere with other families may well be the best for all of you. You yourself will then be with adults while the children find new friends. You may want to choose a 'Special Interest' holiday with the Holiday Fellowship, with the Countrywide Holiday Association or with Galleon Travel; social activities in a house party with the Y.M.C.A., Erna Low, the W.E.A. or at Lee Abbey or Scargill House. If you want more activity the H.F. and C.H.A. cater for this and you will also find suitable (and cheaper) holidays with the Ramblers' Association or through theYouth Hostels Association or in camping holidays at home or abroad. A camping holiday abroad, with perhaps two families going together, with a van and trailer for tents and equipment, can be a real adventure with good planning. The tourist board of the country you want can usually provide a list of camping sites, and the magazine *Popular Camping* will tell you all about hiring equipment. You can also get an A.A. travel route if you are a member. France, Portugal and Italy have well equipped two-star camps.

If you all prefer the idea of a farm holiday with plenty of freedom, country interests and good food, in a friendly environment, study the *Farm Holiday Guide*, which gives a list of farms and country guest houses (25p). It covers Britain county by county, giving furnished accommodation, village inns, camping sites, canal cruises, caravan holidays and places where children are especially welcome.

For children going alone there are many active holiday suggestions. Where supervision is included the cost per week may sometimes be high, but in the higher age groups independent community and athletic holidays are well catered for. Nearly all of the organizations mentioned have special arrangements of this kind. The Council for Colony Holidays is extending its work rapidly. Catering for the nine to fourteen age group it is now planning to take older children and it has the considerable advantage of having its holidays arranged in many parts of the country. The cost is about £17 for twelve days and this includes supervision.

Coming to the holiday which you must take alone, a happy and friendly atmosphere is going to matter a good deal to you. There are plenty of holidays where you can find yourself very much on your own if you are not an actively good mixer, so choose the organizations known for their friendliness. If you have a woman friend, more adventurous plans may be possible and you may want to go abroad. There are holiday centres in many countries, but if you prefer something rather unusual the British India Steam Navigation Co. run school cruises with special accommodation for adult holiday makers. You can join the lectures and enjoy the youthful liveliness of your companions on the voyage and do sight-seeing according to the programme. If you want a summer school with new interests you will find both men and women joining in the lectures and practical work, according to the subject you select. The extramural departments of most universities run summer schools, charging about nine guineas a week all in. The W.E.A. do the same. There are also 'digs' for archaeology students, and painting holidays have become very popular. Urchfont Manor, Devizes; Braziers Park, Ipsden; and Wedgwood Memorial College, near Stoke on Trent, all have programmes if you write to them. Cruse Holiday List for its members has many interesting ideas giving children's holidays, with or without mother, details of work camps, paid work in holiday centres, recuperative holidays in quiet surroundings. *Pets Welcome* and *Self Catering Holidays* are useful booklets.

Whatever you decide, the important thing is to try to avoid places and situations which leave you unhappy in your own company and an embarrassment to others. With sensible choosing this need not happen and your holiday can become one of the happiest memories of your year.

For some of you with an adventurous spirit the idea of emigrating may be the answer to the life of widowhood. If this is so the whole matter needs to be considered very realistically. Some brief details of the widow's position in other countries is given in our International Appendix. Names and addresses of women's clubs to contact are also given. Pension transfer, working possibilities, health, housing and medical care are hard-core subjects that must be looked into. Where some widows might have an opportunity of remarriage, for others who are older life in a new country could be more difficult, whereas their children would probably benefit greatly. There is always the possibility of getting domestic work of all kinds as there is the usual shortage in Australia and other countries open to emigration. In this way too a widow without family ties can work her way throughout the continents seeing new places and meeting many people. Domestic work can, however, be hard, and conditions in some areas rough. For young children, emigrating may give them an ideal setting for growing up. For the older ones there is the need to have a career or training before leaving England. Assisted passages are obtainable in some cases, but friends at the other end are important for the business of settling in. Children can sometimes travel under special subsidized schemes. One of the biggest problems is housing, so thought must be given to this too. It is important to bear in mind that, however irritated people may be by British weather, or even Britain's income tax, there are nevertheless certain big advantages in living in the British Isles. The woman who decides to emigrate must therefore have in her character a high degree of adaptability if she is to make a success of it.

The Appendix gives the necessary addresses.

In this chapter we have attempted both to draw on the widow's resources and to suggest ways of enriching what she feels is a difficult and impoverished life. If, after contemplating the possibilities, she still feels a crippling inertia it will be necessary to go deeper to find the strength to carry on. Too many widows have said, 'Life has become pointless, why go on?'

I should like to suggest that there are clearly-marked signposts which, if followed, lead the way to recovery. First there has to be the wish, however transient, to find the way to better things. It is the beginning of hope, that basic ingredient for all life. From it confidence and belief develop, and the certainty that in spite of all evidence to the contrary, good is in us and around us offering support. In such a situation of positive thinking we cease to be dreamers and accept fully our present lot. It is the material from which we are to build our future, whether long or short in time. The remarkable discovery we can make is that love has not deserted us, and that it is available to us now in a new way. Our own willingness to love and to give in the world about us is the secret of recovery and the new beginning.

APPENDIX

Addresses and Sources of Information

Chapter 2 (pages 8–20)

Anatomy, Inspector of, Alexander Fleming House, Elephant and Castle, London SE1
British Legion, Headquarters, 49 Pall Mall, London SW1 (clothing disposal)
Caravan Information Service, Pembroke House, Wellesley Road, Croydon, Surrey
Caravan Club, 65 South Molton Street, London W1
Church Army Clothing Disposal Department, 105 Melville Road, London NW10
Circle Trust, 25 Camberwell Grove, London SE5 (clothing disposal)
Consumers' Association, 14 Buckingham Street, London WC2
    publications: *What to do when someone dies*; *Arranging a Funeral*
Cruse, Richmond, Surrey
Cyclists' Touring Club, 13 Spring Street, London W2
New Bridge, St Botolph's Church, Aldersgate Street, London EC1 (clothing disposal)
Overseas Group, Department of Health and Social Security, Newcastle upon Tyne
Oxfam, Oxford (clothing disposal)
Personal Application Department, Principal Probate Registry, Somerset House, London WC2
Toc H Headquarters, 15 Trinity Square, London EC3
Women Drivers' Association Ltd, Ewhurst Place, Ewhurst, Surrey
Women's Royal Voluntary Service, Headquarters, 17 Old Park Lane, London W1 (clothing disposal)

Chapter 3 (pages 21–32)

British Legion (men and women), Headquarters, 49 Pall Mall, London SW1
    publication: *British Legion Pension Guide*
British Red Cross Society, Headquarters, 14–15 Grosvenor Crescent, London SW1
Caring for the Widow, Cruse publication: (for enrolled members only) Richmond, Surrey Department of Health and Social Security, Alexander Fleming House, Elephant and Castle, London SE1
Forces' Help Society, 122 Brompton Road, London SW3
International Social Service of Great Britain, 39 Brixton Road, London SW9. King's Fund Centre, 24 Nutford Place, London W1.
National Insurance Commissioner (supplementary benefits only) 6 Grosvenor Gardens, London SW1; 23 Melville Street, Edinburgh 3; 7 Park Place, Cardiff
R.A.F. Benevolent Fund, 67 Portland Place, London W1
Regimental Associations: addresses from Ministry of Defence, Whitehall, London SW1
Royal Naval Benevolent Trust, High Street, Brompton, Gillingham, Kent
Soldiers', Sailors' and Airmen's Families Association, 27 Queen Anne's Gate, London SW1
War Pensioners' Welfare Service, 194 Euston Road, London NW1

The following books include some which are now out of print but which can be borrowed from the library.

BOOKS WRITTEN BY WIDOWS

When you are a Widow, by Clarissa Start (Concordia, 1972)
Grief and how to live with it, by Sarah Morris (Allen & Unwin, 1971)
Learning to live as a Widow, by Marion Langer (Julian Messner, NY)
Gift from the Sea, by Anne Morrow Lindbergh (Chatto & Windus, 1955)
You can start all over, by Marjorie Roulston (The World's Work, 1951)
In the Springtime of the Year, by Susan Hill (Hamish Hamilton, 1974)

FAMILY

The Marriage Book, by Heather Jenner (Duckworth, 1964)
Fatherless Families, by Margaret Wynn (Joseph, 1970)
The World of the Formerly Married, by Morton Hunt (Allen Lane, 1971)
Troubles of Children and Parents, by Susan Isaacs (Methuen, 1969)
Give your Child a Chance, by Bruce Kemble (Pan, 1972) (on education)
Children under Stress, by Sula Wolff (Allen Lane, 1969)
Feeling and Perception in Young Children, by Len Chaloner (Tavistock, 1963)
The Child's World, by Phyllis Hostler (Penguin, 1969)
Adoption, by Margaret Kornitzer (Putnam & Co, 1968)
Your Child from Five to Twelve, Prof. R. S. Illingworth (BMA)
Revolution in Learning, (the pre-school child) Maya Pines (Allen Lane, 1969)
School Holiday Activities, how to organise them. 15p from Case Publications, 17 Jackson's Lane, Billericay, Essex.
Something to Do, by Septima (Puffin books, 1966)
Looking and Finding, by Geoffrey Grigson (Carousel, 1971)
Baby and Child Care, by Dr Benjamin Spock (Four Square, 1969)
When to call the Doctor, and what to do while waiting, by Claire Rayner (Corgi, 1972)
Home Nursing and Family Health, by Claire Rayner (Corgi, 1967)
Children's Parties and Games for a Rainy Day, by Ursula Moray Williams (Corgi, 1972)
A Career for your Son, by Henry Woolland (Corgi, 1969)

HELPFUL BOOKS

Peace from Nervous Suffering, by Dr Claire Weekes (Angus & Robertson, 1972)
Self-Help for your Nerves, by Dr Claire Weekes (Angus & Robertson, 1962)
Anxiety, Nervousness and Depression, by Dr F. R. C. Casson (Corgi, 1971)
The Imprisoned Splendour, by Raynor C. Johnson (Hodder & Stoughton, 1953)
The Prophet, by Kahlil Gibran (Heinemann, 1966)
A Grief Observed, by C. S. Lewis (Faber, 1966)
Healing in Depth, by Culver M. Barker (Hodder & Stoughton, 1972)
Bereavement: studies of grief in adult life, by Colin Murray-Parkes (Tavistock publications, 1973)
Life begins at Death, by Leslie Weatherhead (Denholm House Press, 1969)
Prescription for Anxiety, by Leslie Weatherhead (Hodder & Stoughton, 1956)
Hereafter, by David Winter (Hodder & Stoughton, 1972)
Dying, by John Hinton (Penguin, 1971)

Death, Grief and Mourning, by Geoffrey Gorer (Cresset Press, 1965)
The Pastoral Care of the Bereaved, by Norman Autton (SPCK, 1967)
Is Death the End, by P. and S. Phillips (Corgi, 1972)
Questions on our Mind (mental illness), National Association for Mental Health
    publication.
When Death comes Home (on losing a child), by Simon Stephens (Mowbrays,
    1972)
Explaining Death to Children, by E. A. Grollman (Boston, The Beacon Press, 1967)

GENERAL

Collector's Luck, by Stowers Johnson (J. M. Dent, 1968)
Collecting Man, by John Bedford (Macdonald, 1968) also *Restoring Junk*, *More
    looking in Junk Shops* and *Still looking for Junk*, (1969)
Antiques of the Future, by J. Mackay (Studio Vista, 1970)
Upholstery and Soft Furnishings by V. J. Taylor (Corgi, 1971)
Beauty for the Over 30's, by Zita Aiden (Corgi, 1971)
A Career at Forty, by Madeleine Bingham (Corgi, 1971)
One Woman's Garden, by Elizabeth Coxhead (J. M. Dent, 1971)
How to Cheat at Gardening, by Hazel Evans (Ebury Press, 1971)
Buying Secondhand, (Consumers Association, 1967)
Economical Meat Cookery, by Helen Tullberg (Arrow Books, 1973)
No Time to Cook Book, by Hilda Finn (Corgi, 1967)
Easy Cooking for One or Two, by Louise Davies (Penguin, 1972)
Cut your Motoring Costs, by John Mills (Corgi, 1972)
The Change of Life, by Muriel F. Landau (Corgi, 1971)
The Bonus Years, by Sylvia Duncan (Elek Books, 1970)
    For those with elderly parents:
Living with Old Age, by Betty Ingleby and Margaret Yorath (Robert Hale)

Chapter 6 (pages 50–63)

Advertising Standards Authority Ltd, 1 Bell Yard, London WC2
Brentford Nylons, Brentford, Middx
British United Provident Association, Kingmaker House, New Barnet.

CASH & CARRY AND DISCOUNT BUYING
    Baker, F. P., & Co., 10 Warwick Street, London W1
    Better Buying Service, 56 Grosvenor Street, London W1
    Country Gentlemen's Association Ltd, (C.G.A.) 54 Regent Street, London W1
    Dron, John, Ltd, 6 Highgate High Street, London N6
    N.R.V.W. Ltd (reconditioned refrigerators), 13 High Street, London N8

Corporation of Insurance Brokers, 15 St Helens Place, London EC3
Exchange and Mart, Pembroke House, Wellesley Road, Croydon, Surrey
Good Housekeeping Institute Ltd, Chestergate House, Vauxhall Bridge Road,
    London SW1
Hairdressing Council, 39 Grafton Way, London W1
Hospital Service Plan, Tavistock House South, Tavistock Square, London WC1
Income Tax, Special Commissioners of, Turnstile House, 94 High Holborn,
    London WC1
Nylons Unlimited, Bath

Chapter 7 (pages 64–82)

Building Centres:
  26 Store Street, London WC1E 7BT (for general information on problems)
  The Building Centre of N. Ireland, 4 Arthur Place, Belfast BT1 4HJ
  Engineering & Building Centre, Broad Street, Birmingham B1 2DB
  Building Centre, Colston Avenue, The Centre, Bristol BS1 4TW
  Building Centre, 15–16 Trumpington Street, Cambridge CB2 1QD
  Building Information Centre, Dept of Architecture & Planning, Earl Street, Coventry CV1 5SE
  The Building Centre of Scotland, 6 Newton Terrace, Glasgow G3 7PF
  Liverpool Building & Design Centre, Hope Street, Liverpool L1 9BR
  The Building Centre, 113–115 Portland Street, Manchester M1 6FB
  Midland Design & Building Centre, Mansfield Road, Nottingham NG1 3FE
  The Building Centre, Grosvenor House, 18–20 Cumberland Place, Southampton SO1 2BD
  The Building Information Centre, College of Building & Commerce, Stoke Road, Shelton, Stoke-on-Trent ST4 2DG

British Carpet Centre, Dorland House, 14–16 Regent Street, London SW1Y 4PL
British Wood Preserving Association, Suite 71, 62 Oxford Street, London W1N 9WD
Building Cost Information Service and Building Maintenance Cost Information Service (sponsored by Royal Institute of Chartered Surveyors), 47 Tothill Street, London SW1H 9LH
Building Research Advisory Service, Building Research Station, Garston, Watford, Herts, WD2 7JR
Construction Industry Research & Information Association, Old Queen Street House, 6 Storey's Gate, London SW1 (also CIRIA Guide to Sources of Information)
Extending your House. Consumers' Association
Handyman Which? Back numbers, 60p each, Consumers' Association, Subscription Department, Caxton Hill, Herts.
H.M. Stationery Office, Mail Orders, P.O. Box 569, London SE1 9NH and Regional Offices
Institute of Plumbing, Scottish Mutual House, North Street, Hornchurch, Essex, RM11 1RU
Institution of Heating & Ventilating Engineers, 49 Cadogan Square, London SW1X OJB
Loft Conversions: Elite Loft Conversion Ltd, Holden House, Holden Road, Leigh, Lancs.
Ministry for Housing & Construction, Department of the Environment, 2 Marsham Street, SW1P 3EB
National Federation of Building Trades' Employers, 82 Cavendish Street, London W1
National Federation of Master Painters, 40 King Street West, Manchester 3
National Inspection Council for Electrical Installation Contracting, Trafalgar

Buildings, 1 Charing Cross, London SW1A 2DT
North West Securities Ltd, North West House, City Road, Chester; 1 Regent Street, London W1
Royal Institution of Chartered Surveyors, 12 Great George Street, London SW1 (Sales office for publications through post, 29 Lincoln's Inn Fields, London WC2A 3RD)
Solid Fuel Advisory Service, Hobart House, Grosvenor Place, London SW1X 7AE
Thornfield, G. Ltd, 267 Pentonville Road, London N1 (discount buying)

HOME BUYING AND SELLING

Buying and selling a House; Cruse Fact Sheet, and booklet published by National Council of Social Service, 26 Bedford Square, London WC1; Legal Side of Buying a House, *Which?*, September 1968
Building Societies:
  Abbey National, Abbey House, Baker Street, London NW1
  Chelsea and South London, 110 King's Road, London SW3
  Church of England, 6 New Bridge Street, London EC4
  Civil Service, 26 Caxton Street, London SW1
  Co-operative Permanent, New Oxford House, High Holborn, London WC1
  NALGO, 8 Harewood Row, London NW1
  Property Owners, 4 Cavendish Place, London W1

Housing Associations, Societies and Departments:
  National Federation of Housing Societies, 86 Strand, London WC2
  Abbeyfield Societies, Head Office, 22 Nottingham Place, London W1
  British Churches Housing Trust, Church of England Social Responsibility Department, Church House, London SW10
  Carr/Gomm Society Ltd, 36 Gomm Road, London SE16
  Church Army Housing Ltd, 185 Marylebone Road, London NW10
  Civil Service Housing Association Ltd, 26 Caxton Street, London SW1
  Douglas Haig Memorial Homes, Alban Dobson House, Green Lane, Morden, Surrey
  Edith Urch Housing Schemes, 68 Warwick Way, London SW1 (30 houses)
  Enfield Housing Association, 1 Cecil Court, London Road, Enfield, Middx
  Harding Housing Association Ltd, 5 Hogarth Place, London SW5
  Housing Action Centre, 264 Portobello Road, London W10
  Housing Association for Officers' Families, 341 London Road, Mitcham, Surrey
  Housing Centre Trust, 13 Suffolk Street, London SW1
  Housing Corporation, Sloane Square House, Holbein Place, London SW1
  Mutual Households Association Ltd, 41 Kingsway, London WC2
  Samuel Lewis Dwellings Trust, 10 Great James Street, London WC1
  Shelter Housing Aid Centre (incorporating the Catholic Housing Aid Society) 189a Old Brompton Road, London SW5
  United Women's Homes Association Ltd, 3 Vandon Street, London SW1
  W.R.V.S. Housing Schemes, and Furniture Department, 17 Old Park Lane, London W1
  Widow's Friend Society, 450 Edgware Road, London W2
    Flatlets 2 Warwick Road, London W5,
  Flatshare, 213 Piccadilly, London W1 (for professional people)
  London Accommodation Bureau, Berkertex House, 309 Oxford Street, London W1
Retire and Enjoy It by Cecil Chisholm (Penguin Books edition, 1961)

Save and Prosper, 4 Great St Helens, London EC3P 3EP
Share-a-Flat Ltd, 175 Piccadilly, London W1

  Daltons Weekly, Windsor Avenue, Merton, London SW19
  Homefinder and Small Property Guide, 199 Strand, London WC2
  London Property Letter, 114 New Bond Street, London W1

Chapter 8 (pages 83–98)

Anglo Scandinavian Educational Holidays, 28a York Street, London W1H 1FE
British Council, Headquarters, 65 Davies Street, London W1
British Council for the Rehabilitation of the Disabled, Tavistock House (South),
    Tavistock Square, London W1
British Federation of University Women, Crosby Hall, Cheyne Walk, London
    SW3
Careers for Girls and Women, published by Women's Employment Federation,
    251 Brompton Road, London SW3
Central Training Council in Child Care, Home Office, Horseferry Road, London
    SW1
Cheshire Foundation Homes for the Sick, 7 Market Mews, London W1
Church of England Social Responsibility Department, Church House, London
    SW1
Civil Service Commission, Standard House, Northumberland Avenue, London
    WC2
Clothing Institute Ltd, 17 Henrietta Street, London WC2
College of Deaf Welfare, 321 Green Lanes, Manor House, London N4
Cruse publications: *Buying a Business*; *Training*; *Market Research*; *Domestic Op-
    portunities*; *Work for Widows*
Dressing for Success by Jean Rook (J. M. Dent, 1968)
Employment, Department of, 8 St James's Square, London SW1
Employment Fellowship, Drayton House, Gordon Street, London W1
En Famille Agency Ltd, Westbury House, Queen's Lane, Arundel, Sussex
Family Service Units (Head Office), 207 Marylebone Road, London NW1
Foyle's Lecture Agency, 119 Charing Cross Road, London WC2
Gabbitas-Thring Educational Trust Ltd, 6/8 Sackville Street, London W1
Gentlewomen's Work and Help Society, Ralli Buildings, Stanley Street, Manches-
    ter 3
Hillcroft College, South Bank, Surbiton, Surrey
Hotel & Catering Institute, 191 Trinity Road, London SW1
Institute of Personnel Management, 5 Winsley Street, London W1
Institutional Management Association, 324 Grays Inn Road, London WC1
Lady, The, 40 Bedford Street, London WC2
London School of Economics, Houghton Street, London WC2
Manpower Ltd, 100 Notting Hill Gate, London N11, and branches in many towns
    (jobs for women too)
Marks & Spencer Ltd (Staff Management Office), Michael House, Baker Street,
    London W1
National Association for Mental Health, 39 Queen Anne Street, London W1
National Association of Women's Clubs, 26 Bedford Square, London WC1
National College for Training of Youth Leaders, Humberstone Drive, Leicester
National Corporation for the Care of Old People, Nuffield Lodge, Regents Park,
    London NW1

National Council of Social Service, 26 Bedford Square, London WC1
National Extension College, Cambridge
National Housewives' Register, 39 Chawn Park Drive, Pedmore, Stourbridge, Worcs.
National Institute of Adult Education, 35 Queen Anne Street, London W1
National Society for the Prevention of Cruelty to Children, 1 Riding House Street, London W1
Nursing Recruitment Service, 6 Cavendish Square, London W1
Over Forty Association for Women Workers, Grosvenor Gardens House, London SW1
Priscilla Lobley Flower Kits Ltd, Thorpe Lodge, Ealing Green, London W5 5EN
Prison Service (training for), Establishment Division 3, Home Office, Romney House, Marsham Street, London SW1
Probation and Aftercare Department, Home Office, 73 Great Peter Street, London SW1
Registrar of Companies, Companies House, 55 City Road, London EC1
Retirement (Chapter 4) by R. G. Russell and Boswell Taylor (Hodder & Stoughton, 1965)
Royal College of Midwives, 15 Mansfield Street, London W1
Royal Institute of Public Health and Hygiene, 28 Portland Place, London W1N 4DE
Royal National Institute for the Blind, 224 Great Portland Street, London W1
Society of Chiropodists, 8 Wimpole Street, London W1
Townswomen's Guilds, National Union of, 2 Cromwell Place, London SW7
Teacher, The, Derbyshire House, St Chad's Street, London WC1
Teacher's World, Montague House, Russell Square, London WC1
Times Educational Supplement, The, Printing House Square, London EC4
Training Council for Teachers of the Mentally Handicapped, Alexander Fleming House, London SE1
Trust Houses Forte Ltd, 166 High Holborn, London WC1
Universal Aunts Ltd, 36 Walpole Street, London SW3
Woman's Own, Tower House, Southampton Street, London WC2
Women's Employment Federation, 251 Brompton Road, London SW3
Women's Home Industries, 85a Pimlico Road, London SW1
Women's Institutes, National Federation of, 39 Eccleston Street, London SW1
Workers' Educational Association, 9 Upper Berkeley Street, London W1
Working Wonders by P. Williams (Hodder & Stoughton, 1969)
Young Women's Christian Association, 2 Weymouth Street, London W1

Chapter 9 (pages 99–118)

BOOKS ABOUT CHILDREN

The Child, the Family and the Outside World by D. W. Winnicott (Penguin, 1964)
Child Care and the Growth of Love by J. Bowlby (Penguin, 1953)
A Parents' Guide to Sex Education by C. Rayner (Corgi Books, 1968)
Caring for Children in Hospital (King's Fund Centre report, 1974)

BOOKS FOR CHILDREN AND YOUNG PEOPLE

Peter and Caroline by S. Hegeler (Tavistock, 1967); an excellent book on sex and childbirth for children
He and She by Kenneth Barnes (older boys and girls) (Penguin, 1962)
Money Wise by Gilda Lund (Mills & Boon, 1966); getting, keeping and spending money—for older boys

The Way You Are by Anne Allen (for girls) (Hale, 1963)
Sex and Teenagers In Love by L. Barnett (Denholm House Press, 1967)
Pot or Not? A Plain Guide to Drug Dependence by A. J. Wood (B.M.A., 1967)
Brook Advisory Centre for Young People, 55 Dawes Street, London SE17

Advisory Centre for Education, Trumpington Street, Cambridge
Careers Guide, Central Youth Employment Executive (H.M.S.O., annual
amendments by subscription)
Careers Research and Advisory Centre, Bateman Street, Cambridge
Occupational Guidance Units: Employment Exchanges have list; service free

Child Guidance Clinics—list from National Association for Mental Health, 39
Queen Anne Street, London W1
Children's Bazaar Ltd (sale of good clothes), 162c Sloane Street, London SW1
Children's Market (sale of good clothes), 29 Holland Street, London W8
Children's clothes free on allocation from W.R.V.S. Clothing Depots; Citizens'
Advice Bureau or Cruse will advise
Cruse, Richmond, Surrey
publications: *The Widow's Child* by Margaret Torrie (giving addresses for aid);
Parents' Circle Reports for Members; Boarding Schools List
Girl Guides Association, 17 Buckingham Palace Road, London SW1

Anglo-Austrian Society, 139 Kensington High Street, London W8
Anglo-Continental Educational Holidays, 28a York Street, London W1
Cruse Holiday List
Educational Interchange Council, 43 Russell Square, London WC1
Erna Low Travel Service Ltd, 7 Bute Street, London SW7—special youth
holidays and children without parents.

National Adoption Society, 47a Manchester Street, London W1
National Council for One-Parent Families, 255 Kentish Town Road, London
NW5
National Society of Children's Nurseries, Montgomery Hall, Kennington Oval,
London SE11
Nicholson's London Guide, R. Nicholson, 3 Goodwins Court, St Martins Lane,
London WC2 and *London Girl* (40p each)
Opportunity Group (birth to seven for handicapped children and their
mothers), affiliated to Pre-school Playgroups
Pregnancy Advisory Service, 40 Margaret Street, London W1
Pre-retirement Association, 194 Clapham Park Road, London SW4 7DU
Pre-school Playgroups Association, 87a High Street, London SE1; and 304
Maryhill Road, Glasgow NW
Release (drugs), 1 Elgin Avenue, London W9 3PR
Save the Children Fund, 29 Queen Anne's Gate, London SW1
Scout Association, 25 Buckingham Palace Road, London SW1
Task Force, 2/8 Victoria Street, London SW1
Vacation Work International, 9 Park End Street, Oxford
What's On in London for Young People, 5–6 Argyll Street, London W1
Working Association of Mothers, Mrs Diana Priestley, 22 Victoria Road, Ted-
dington, Middlesex.

Young People's Consultative Centre, Tavistock Institute, Belsize Lane, London NW3

Chapter 10 (pages 119–129) and Chapter 11 (pages 130–146)

BOOKS

The Marriage Book by Heather Jenner (Duckworth, 1964)
Sexual Life after Sixty by Dr Isadore Ruben (Allen & Unwin, 1966)
Sex in Marriage by D. W. Baruch and H. Miller (Allen & Unwin, 1963)

CULTURAL AND SOCIAL ORGANIZATIONS

Babyminders, 126 Wigmore Street, London W1
Cambridge House Literacy Scheme, 131 Camberwell Road, London SE5
Canuspa, 32 Dale Grove, London N12
English-Speaking Union, 37 Charles Street, London W1
Eros Escort & Guide Service, 213 Piccadilly, London W1
Historical Association, 59a Kennington Park Road, London SE11
International Friendship League, 3 Creswick Road, London W3
London Appreciation Society, 8 Scarsdale Villas, London W8
National Adult School Union, Drayton House, Gordon Street, London WC1
National Association of Women's Clubs, 26 Bedford Square, London WC1
National Book League, 7 Albemarle Street, London W1
Problem Ltd, 179 Vauxhall Bridge Road, London SW1
Royal Overseas League, Overseas House, Park Place, St James's Street, London SW1
Ryder Domestics, 36 Earls Court Road, London W8
Toc H Women's Group, 42 Crutched Friars, London EC3
Victoria League for Commonwealth Friendship, 38 Chesham Place, London SW1
Workers' Educational Association, 9 Upper Berkeley Street, London W1

Local Branches of the following can be found through the local Citizens' Advice Bureau or the notice board of your public library:
Women's Institute, Townwomen's Guild, Mothers' Union, Y.W.C.A., British Legion, Red Cross, W.R.V.S., Soroptimists

HELPING OTHERS: ADVISORY SOCIETIES

Citizens' Advice Bureaux
Local Councils of Social Service
National Council of Social Service, 26 Bedford Square, London WC1
Social Work Advisory Service, 26 Bloomsbury Way, London WC1

HOLIDAYS WITH OR WITHOUT THE CHILDREN

Council for Colony Holidays, Shepherd House, Hanley Swan, Worcestershire
Countrywide Holiday Association, Birch Heys, Cromwell Range, Manchester 14
Cruse Holiday List, Cruse, Richmond, Surrey
Holiday Fellowship Ltd, 142 Great North Way, London NW4
Junior Tourism, 52 Chester Square, London SW1
Lee Abbey, Lynton, North Devon

Scargill House, Kettlewell, Skipton, Yorks
Tourist Information Centre, 64 St James's Street, London SW

Pets Welcome and *Children Welcome* (20p each), Herald Advisory Services, 23A
   Brighton Road, South Croydon, Surrey (annually)
Self Catering Holidays (30p) and *Bed and Breakfast and Evening Meal* (25p), Star-
   fish Books, Cobham, Surrey (annually)

POLITICAL PARTIES
   Conservative Central Office, 32 Smith Square, London SW1
   Labour Party Headquarters, Transport House, Smith Square, London SW1
   Liberal Party Headquarters, 7 Exchange Court, London WC2

RECREATION
   Conservation Corps, The Council for Nature, Zoological Gardens, Regents
      Park, London NW1 (or through local Natural History Societies)
   English Folk Dance and Song Society, 2 Regents Park Road, London NW1
   Ramblers' Association, 124 Finchley Road, London NW3
   Women's League of Health and Beauty, Headquarters, 45 Rosedene Avenue,
      London SW16
   Youth Hostels Association, 29 John Adam Street, London WC2

RELIGIOUS/PHILOSOPHICAL INTERESTS (for those not belonging to the main
   churches)
   British Humanist Association, 13 Prince of Wales Terrace, London W8
   Baha' I Centre, 27 Rutland Gate, London SW7
   Society of Friends, Friends House, Euston Road, London NW1
   Spiritual Regeneration Movement, Foundation of Great Britain (The Mahari-
      shi), Suite 5, Iddesleigh House, Caxton Street, London SW1

INTERNATIONAL APPENDIX

GREAT BRITAIN
AUSTRALIA
AUSTRIA
BELGIUM
CANADA
CYPRUS
DENMARK
EIRE
FINLAND
FRANCE
WEST GERMANY
HONG KONG
INDIA
ISRAEL
ITALY
JAPAN
MALTA
NETHERLANDS
NEW ZEALAND
NORWAY
SOUTH AFRICA
SPAIN
SWEDEN
SWITZERLAND
TURKEY
U.S.A.

Owing to unavoidable delays in publishing, this information relates to the position
in 1972/3. In order to retain direct comparison in the Appendix the position of
widows in Great Britain is also shown as at 1973. The 1974 rates for Great Britain
are listed in the Addenda on page 185.

The following Questionnaire was used in compiling the International Appendix. We are grateful for the help we have had in gathering information on the widow's position in twenty-five countries from the Embassies and High Commissions in London, and in some cases from the government departments, social science faculties of the universities, and the widows' organizations of individual countries.

QUESTIONNAIRE

1. *Pension* (a) Is there a statutory pension for widow nationals?
   (b) Are there age restrictions?
   (c) Are there insurance contribution restrictions?
   (d) Is there a reciprocal arrangement with Britain?
   (e) Approximate amount of pension at 1973.

2. *Income Tax* (a) Minimum rate for liability?
   (b) Standard rate?
   (c) Is there an earnings rule for widows?
   (d) Is pension taxed with earnings?

3. *Children* (a) Is there a Children's (Orphans') Allowance?
   (b) Approximate amount.
   (c) To what age?
   (d) Is allowance continued if widow remarries?

4. *Housing* (a) Can a widow, with or without children, rent a house or apartment?
   (b) Approximate cost.
   (c) Can she get a mortgage?

5. *Employment* (a) What professional qualifications would allow a widow to take up work immediately?
   (b) What work is readily available without any qualification?
   (c) Standard wage for women?
   (d) Employment authority to consult.

6. *Education* (a) Is it free or fee-paid?
   (b) Main sources of grant-aid for schooling and further education?

7. *Women's Organizations* e.g. Politico-socio (such as National Council of Women)
   Accredited widows' organizations
   International groups
   National social groups (such as Women's Institutes)
   General information bureaux.

8. *British family emergency*
   If husband dies while family is abroad:
   (a) Which authority will help the widow?
   (b) Is any emergency financial help available?
   (c) Can burial take place locally?
   (d) Possible cost of funeral and of transporting deceased home.

General remarks

  Pension categories:

We have given the position of the statutory widow throughout. In Britain and in other countries reviewed *War Widows* receive higher state allowances than other widows. Special help is available for them from service sources and their benevolent funds, with rent allowances and extra funeral grants in some cases.

Industrial Widows also receive higher allowances and conditions as to length of insurance or number of contributions paid are waived. In Britain it is only War Widows and Industrial Widows who are paid a gratuity on remarriage.

  British Family emergency Point 8.

In all cases local interment was said to be possible. If the family wishes the funeral to take place in Britain the cost of the arrangements for transport and interment amount to approximately £500.

  Positive points

We have indicated some positive points in the policy of other countries towards widows and their children in italic type.

GREAT BRITAIN

Statutory Widows' PENSION on contribution qualification: Widow's Allowance for first 26 weeks of £10·85 a week (from Oct. 1973). After 26 weeks, widowed mothers and those aged 50 or more receive £7·75; age-related pension for widows aged 40–50, widow's basic pension £2·33. Widow cannot receive more than one statutory benefit at a time, but Supplementary Allowances are payable to her on means test if not in full-time work: rate for single householder £7·50, plus allowance for rent and for dependants. For those in full-time work Family Income Supplement brings household weekly income up to £20, awarded for 26 weeks at a time. Department of Health and Social Security, Alexander Fleming House, London SE1.

MEDICAL. National Health Service available to all, not dependent on insurance contributions. Free hospital care, GP and specialist consultations. Free prescriptions for under 15s, over 65s, expectant and nursing mothers, those receiving supplementary benefit: others pay 20p per prescription item, half cost of dental charges to maximum of £10, free eyesight testing with charges for spectacles. Private insurance and medical care for those who wish to pay.

INCOME TAX. Personal allowance of £595 plus allowances for children (£700 for widows over 65). Pension taxed with earnings, except for war pensions in respect of children. Supplementary benefits not taxable. Unified tax rate after deductions starts at 30%.

CHILDREN. Widow receives £4·00 a week for each child under 16 (or 19 if still in full-time education). This includes Family Allowance payable to second and subsequent children. Dept. of Health and Social Security. Only the Family Allowance continues if widow remarries.

HOUSING costs continue to rise. Rent allowances from local councils for tenants of private landlords or housing associations. Also scheme of rent rebates for council tenants, new town tenants and private house owners with income below £30 a week. Supplementary benefits take rents into consideration.

EMPLOYMENT. Opportunities for women to train or retrain in professions and trades through colleges, government training centres and specialist courses. Part-time work possibilities in many fields. From 1975 women are to receive equal pay with men for comparable jobs. No earnings rule for widows but levied on pensioners between 60 and 65.

EDUCATION is free from age 5, limited number of free pre-school playgroups with priority given to one-parent families. Preparatory and 'public schools' are fee-paid, approximately £1,000 a year, assistance from scholarships, charitable trusts and benevolent funds. Local authority grants on parents' means test for university and college students. Open University courses by correspondence and radio for all ages.

AUSTRALIA

(Exchange rate at May 1973:
£1 = 1·8 Australian dollars)

Widow's PENSION is paid on means test to widowed mothers and to those widowed at 50 or more. Also payable at 45 to widow whose mother's allowance has ended. Residence qualifications are necessary for benefits, but under reciprocal arrangements with Britain residence in the UK is counted towards qualification. No insurance contribution restrictions. Maximum pension (1973) 21·50 Aus. dollars per week. Federal Pension Authority: Dept. of Social Security, PO Box 1, Woden, ACT 2606. Also State departments.

Contributions to registered MEDICAL benefit funds cover partial cost of doctors' fees, medicines and hospital care. Pensioners and their dependants receive free medical and pharmaceutical benefits. Free and comprehensive Health Centres planncd.

INCOME TAX on taxable income above 1,040 Aus. dollars. Pension not taxed with earnings as Widow's Pension is paid subject to means test on income and assets.

Additional pension for dependent CHILDREN up to maximum of 21·50 Aus. dollars a week if mother's income is low. Paid up to age 16, longer if student, subject to annual means test. State Dept of Capital Territory Social Welfare Section is at Akuna House, Akuna Street, Canberra City, ACT 2601.

Most HOUSING Departments allow rebates on rents for pensioners in government accommodation. Mortgages available, generally more difficult for 'single' person to get housing loan. State Housing Commission in each State. Dept of Capital Territory (Housing Branch): Qantas House, London Circuit, Canberra City, ACT 2601.

WORK opportunities depend on labour market. Unqualified person takes pot luck. Medical and nursing qualifications from UK are recognised, teaching qualifications may have to be supplemented locally. No earnings rule for widows. Specific job information from: Dept of Labour, 125 Swanston Street, Melbourne, Victoria 3000. Good local employment agencies exist.

EDUCATION for children is free, private schools only at parent's choice. Education Depts in each state. Commonwealth Dept of Education, ACT Education Services Branch, Scarborough House, Phillip, ACT 2606. Scholarships from State and Federal Education Depts, assistance for books and clothing from welfare depts.

Women's Organizations etc.

National Council of Women of Australia, 33 Greengate Road, Killara, NSW.
YWCA, 68 Powlett Street, E. Melbourne, Victoria 3002.
Women's Liberation.

Royal Commonwealth Society, Royal Overseas League, Victoria League and
  English Speaking Union have branches in capital cities.
Council for Single Mother and her Child.
Civilian Widows' Assoc., 11 Fisher Street, Petersham, Sydney, and 98 Victoria
  Street, N. Richmond 3121, Victoria.
Sydney Legacy Offices, 144 Castlereagh Street, Sydney, NSW. (Much help to ser-
  vice families and widows.)
The Good Neighbour Council, 67 Castlereagh Street, Sydney, NSW.
Citizens' Advice Bureaux.

BRITISH FAMILY EMERGENCY

Help from British High Commission (Commonwealth Avenue, Canberra) and discretionary financial assistance from State Welfare authorities. Reciprocal arrangements on social security (DHSS leaflet SA 5) do not cover medical services and
expenses cannot be reimbursed.

AUSTRIA

(Exchange rate at May 1973:
£1 = 50·85 schillings)

Widow's PENSION paid on contribution qualification. No age restriction but
subject to earnings rule. *Gratuity of 70 monthly pension payments to widow on
remarriage.* Amount is calculated as 60% of husband's pension entitlement, paid
monthly 14 times a year (60 weeks). Pensions adjusted each year to cost of living.
State Pensions Authority: Hauptverband der oesterreichischen Sozialversicher-
ungstraeger, Rossauer Laende 3, 1092 Wien 9.
  MEDICAL insurance scheme contributions cover partial medical and hospital
costs, not dentists.
  INCOME TAX starts at £350 annual income. Pension taxed with earnings.
  CHILDREN of widow receive Orphan's Allowance equal to 40% of widow's
pension (60% for full orphan) payable to 18, or 26 if student, indefinitely for disabled child. *Allowance is continued if widow remarries.* Local Youth Welfare
Authority (Jugendamt).
  HOUSING is scarce in many areas. Advice from local Housing Dept of area in
which house is sought (Wohnungsamt).
  All qualifications for professional EMPLOYMENT must be Austrian. Domestic and factory work according to labour market. Wages not equal to men, earnings rule for widows. Jobs found through local Labour Exchange (Arbeitsamt), no
employment agencies.
  EDUCATION mainly in state schools with minimal attendance fee, relief for
lower paid. School books and fares are free, age 6 to 15. No afternoon school,
*working mothers can send children to Youth Centres for lunch and afternoon or hol-
iday occupation for small fee.* State grants and provincial govt. grants through local
authority for further education (on means test). Music Academy has status of university. Federal Ministry of Education (Bundesministerium für Unterricht) Mino-
ritenplatz 5, 1010 Wien 1.

WOMEN'S ORGANIZATIONS ETC.
Political parties have women's groups.
YWCA, many branches.
Supportive Catholic groups, contact through local church (over 90% of Austrians are Catholic).
General information from Town Halls.

BRITISH FAMILY EMERGENCY
Advice and possible funds from British Embassy. Reciprocal arrangements with Britain (DHSS leaflet SA 25) cover widow's benefit but not medical costs. However, free hospital treatment could be arranged in emergency. British subject needs work permit. Doctors, lawyers, teachers, etc. would need to retrain before they could be employed.

BELGIUM

(Exchange rate at May 1973:
£1 = 98·50 francs)

PENSION paid to widowed mothers and widows of 45 or older whose husbands worked for Belgian employers and were insured under one or other of the separate schemes for wage earners, seamen, mineworkers and civil servants. Widow of foreign worker working for Belgian employer in Belgium has same advantages for pension, children's allowance, social security. Amount is calculated as 80% of retirement pension if husband had retired, 60% if not. *Two years' pension paid as gratuity if widow remarries. Holiday bonus paid to pensioners including widows.*

MEDICAL insurance contributions cover partial cost of treatment and total cost of hospital care.

INCOME TAX minimum rate approximately Belgian Fr. 75,000, with further allowance for dependants. Pension taxed with earnings.

Orphan's benefit paid for CHILDREN if father worked in Belgium for Belgian company and was insured. Paid in the form of increased Family Allowance to age 14, 25 if student or disabled. Office national d'Allocation Familiale, rue de Trêves, 1040 Bruxelles.

HOUSING. A small apartment for two people costs Belgian Fr. 2,500–3,000 per month in rent. House purchase arrangements through public notary.

More openings for EMPLOYMENT for women with qualifications. Unqualified shop and factory work, posts as governess to children or companion to elderly people. Wages range from Belgian Fr. 5,000–20,000 per month. Widow cannot work more than 90 hours a month or she loses her pension. Office national d'Emploi, Boulevard de l'Empereur, Bruxelles.

EDUCATION is free, except for private institutions or convents, under Ministère de l'Education nationale, Bruxelles. Grants for further education from Fonds National des Etudes, Cité Administrative, 1000 Bruxelles.

WOMEN'S ORGANIZATIONS ETC.
Information concerning all problems and local branches of women's organizations from Infor-femmes, 29 rue de Bréderode, 1000 Bruxelles.

Widows' organization: Fraternité des Veuves, rue de la Prevoyance 58, 1000 Bruxelles.
Conseil National de Femmes Belges, 16 Avenue de la Toison d'Or, Bruxelles 6.

Discretionary financial help from social security offices. British Embassy at 28 rue
Joseph II, 1040 Bruxelles. British Consular Offices at Antwerp, Ostend, Ghent and
Liège.

CANADA

(Exchange rate at May 1973:
£1 = 2·5465 dollars)

Widow's PENSION provisions cover all residents insured under Canada Pension
Plan. Approximate amount (1973) 18 dollars weekly. (Old Age Pension is 25 dol-
lars weekly). Agreement between UK and Canada on social security (DHSS leaflet
SA 20) does not cover widows' pensions. Income Security Branch and Canada
Pension Plan Branch, Ministry of Health and Welfare, Ottawa, Ontario.

MEDICAL. No national health service, only provincial schemes of hospital insurance. Residents of more than 3 months can be covered. Medical and dental
treatment is very expensive.

An annual INCOME TAX allowance of 1,750 dollars basic personal exemption, plus allowances for medical and charity payments and clothing. Pension
taxed with earnings.

CHILDREN may receive Orphan's allowance of 7 dollars weekly if father's insurance record qualifies, up to age 18, or 25 for students. *Orphan's allowance continues if widow remarries.* Dept of Welfare in each of the 10 provinces. Dept of
National Health and Welfare, Brooke Claxton Building, Ottawa.

HOUSING. Rents vary greatly. Mortgage enquiries to Central Mortgage and
Housing Corporation, Montreal Road, Ottawa.

EMPLOYMENT prospects are better for those with qualifications. Domestic
and factory work according to labour market, mother's helps, seasonal jobs in can-
ning factories and on farms. No earnings rule for widows. Assistant Deputy Minister (Manpower), Dept of Manpower and Immigration, 305 Rideau Street, Ottawa.

EDUCATION can be free or fee-paid. Grants from government support further
education. Dept of Education office in each province. Parts of Canada are French-
speaking or bi-lingual.

Dept of Labour Women's Bureaux in individual provinces.
Ontario Human Rights Commission, 400 University Avenue, Toronto 2.
National Council of Women of Canada, 190 Lisgar Street, Ottawa 4.
YWCA, 571 Jarvis Street, Toronto 5.
Catholic Women's League of Canada, 77 MacLaren Street, Ottawa.
Social Work Adviser, Dept of Health, Office of the Deputy Minister, Toronto 5.
Daughters of England Benevolent Society, 100 John Street, Weston, Ontario.

Parents without Partners, Box 232 Victoria Station, Montreal 6.

BRITISH FAMILY EMERGENCY
Help from nearest British government office and local Welfare agencies. Possible
help with funeral arrangements from Daughters of England Benevolent Soc., also
social support. Widow with typing or nursing skills or up-to-date professional
qualification can take up work (e.g. hairdresser, teacher, cook, doctor, librarian).
Enquiries to local Canada Manpower Center. Family allowance can be paid for
children under 16 if they have been resident in Canada at least 1 year.

CYPRUS

(Exchange rate at May 1973:
£1 = £0·910mils)

PENSION paid on contribution qualification to all widows of insured workers. If
husband died as result of industrial or commuting accident there are no contribution conditions. Amount (1973) is £2·000 weekly (£3·200 mils for Industrial
Widow's Pension) with increases for dependants. Dept of Social Insurance, 7
Byron Avenue, Nicosia, Cyprus.
   INCOME TAX minimum rate for liability is £400. 10% of all earned income including pensions is tax-free, also £100 per annum of chargeable income of over
65's. Pension taxed with earnings.
   CHILDREN'S allowance paid at the rate of £0·900 mils per week for one dependent child, £1·200 for two, £1·500 for three or more. Paid to age 16. Dept of Social
Welfare Services, Nicosia.
   HOUSING. Average rent £10 weekly. Rates are very low. Property can be
bought, aliens need approval of Council of Ministers. Advice from Housing
branch of Dept of Town Planning & Housing, Nicosia. Workers' houses are managed by Municipalities.
   EMPLOYMENT opportunities depend on labour market. Seasonal or part
time work picking and packing potatoes and citrus fruits, also domestic and hotel
work in connection with tourist industry. No earnings rule for widows. Women receive equal pay with men, according to provisions of collective bargaining agreements in different occupations. Employment Services of the District Labour and
Social Insurance Offices.
   EDUCATION is free from age 6 to 13 (to be extended to age 15). Help for
further education from Council of Ministers, also School Boards and Church and
individual Trusts. Ministry of Education, Nicosia, Republic of Cyprus.

WOMEN'S ORGANIZATIONS ETC.
Pancyprian Federation of Women's Organizations (POGO), a national women's
    organization with left wing affiliation working for women's rights and welfare.
Inner Wheel, c/o Constantia Hotel, Famagusta (source of social help).
Poor Relief Organizations (Pholoptohos) operating under church auspices. Help
    with clothing, medicines, school fees, dowries and moral guidance.
Greek Ladies' Association, Limmassol. Runs a Day Nursery for children of work-
    ing mothers.

Greek Ladies' Association, Paphos. Raises funds to help fatherless families, gives
dowries to girls and educational help to boys.
Social Care Organisation, Famagusta.
Social Provident Fund, Ayii Omoloyitae, Nicosia.

BRITISH FAMILY EMERGENCY

Help from Dept of Social Welfare Services, Nicosia, and from British High Commission, Alexander Pallis Street, Nicosia. Emergency medical services obtainable through General Hospital in all main towns. No British doctors or dentists
are practising in Cyprus. Reciprocal arrangements with UK (DHSS leaflet SA
12).

DENMARK

(Exchange rate at May 1973:
£1 = 15·38 Krone)

Statutory PENSION for nationals widowed after their 45th birthday is payable at
age 55, or from age 45 to mother maintaining two or more children under age 18.
*Maintenance Allowance is assessed for younger widows to enable them to raise their
families and undertake training courses*: receipt of regular Maintenance Allowance
entitles widow to statutory Widow's Pension on temporary basis. No contribution
requirements, but from 1973 entitlement to full pension subject to 40 years residence by widow or husband. Maximum is approximately £11 a week, adjusted
twice yearly to cost of living index. Special pension supplement may be awarded.
Ministry of Social Affairs, Slotsholmsgade 6, 1216 Copenhagen K.

MEDICAL care under local Health Insurance Fund (Sygekasse). Covers hospital care, some medicines, clinics. Not dentistry. Danish Health Service, Direc-
torate of Health Insurance Services, Amaliegade 25, 1256 Copenhagen K.

INCOME TAX. Earnings rule for widows receiving full Widows' Pension
applies on annual earnings above 4,600 Kr. Pension taxed with earnings.

All Danish CHILDREN entitled to Family Allowance to age 18, single parents
receive more than married couples. (1,469 Kr quarterly for each child.) If mother
remarries family allowance continues at reduced rate of 920 Kr every three
months. Ministry of Social Affairs.

HOUSING. Rents are high in the towns. Rate relief. Ministry of Housing,
Slotsholmsgade 12, 1216 Copenhagen K.

EMPLOYMENT opportunities depend on whether widow's qualifications are
up-to-date. Unskilled work in factories, also domestic and shop work. Vocational
and training schemes. The local Employment Service is supervised by Ministry of
Labour. Equal pay proposals still controversial.

EDUCATION is free. Further education grants from Exchequer. Ministry of
Education, Frederiksholms Kanal 21, 1220 Copenhagen K.

WOMEN'S ORGANIZATIONS ETC.

The Danish Women's Society, Niels Hemmingsensgade 8–10, 1153 Copenhagen
K.

The National Council of Women of Denmark, same address.
YWCA.

BRITISH FAMILY EMERGENCY
Help from British Embassy, Kastelsvej 38–40, Copenhagen, and 7 British Consulates. Under reciprocal agreement (DHSS leaflet SA 18) visitors to Denmark from Britain can receive urgent medical attention free or for partial reimbursement.

EIRE

Two types of Widows' PENSION, contributory and non-contributory. No age restrictions. For a contributory pension a husband must have paid in for at least four years. Maximum pension for widow without a child dependant is £5·60; for widowed mother the rate is increased by £1·50 a week per child. A non-contributory pension is assessed by means test and number of dependants. Dept of Social Welfare, Phibsboro Tower, Dublin 7.

MEDICAL. The Health Service operates under the Regional Health Boards. Persons insured under the Social Welfare Acts (and their dependants) are entitled to free or partially free medical services, including dental treatment, spectacles and hearing aids.

INCOME TAX standard rate 35p in the £. *A widow gets a personal allowance of £25 more than a single person*, earned income allowance is same as single person. Pension taxed with earnings.

CHILDREN. Mother receives allowances on her own pension (£1·50 a week per child). Family allowances are less than in Britain.

HOUSING can be rented for £8–£9 weekly. For Dublin area apply to Dublin Corporation, elsewhere to County Councils.

A widow can find EMPLOYMENT if she is qualified in any of the professions, or in secretarial or book-keeping work, or is a Civil Servant. Unskilled domestic work, canteens, factory or shop work for £10 to £18 a week. No earnings rule. Employment authority: National Manpower Service, O'Connell Bridge House, Dublin 2.

EDUCATION is free. Primary schooling is in hands of the state, secondary is in private hands, controlled by Religious Orders. Vocational schools also provide secondary education and there are recently-established comprehensive schools. Irish is regarded as first language, English as second.

WOMEN'S ORGANIZATIONS ETC.

Irish Housewives' Association.
Irish Countrywomen's Association.
YWCA.
The National Association of Widows in Ireland, 3 North Earl Street, Dublin 1
  (social and supportive help, job advice).
Association of Widows of Civil Servants.

BRITISH FAMILY EMERGENCY
Discretionary help from nearest Social Welfare office. British Embassy, 39 Merrion Square, Dublin.

FINLAND

(Exchange rate at May 1973:
£1 = 9·92 markka)

Statutory PENSION provisions for widows of 40 to 65 years and widowed mothers. There are conditions regarding duration of marriage. Pension adjusted automatically to cost of living. *Lump sum of one year's pension as gratuity if widow remarries. Holiday bonus paid to mother.* National Pensions Institution, Nordenskioldinkatu 12, 00250 Helsinki 25.

MEDICAL costs largely covered by industrial and motor insurance provisions and Sickness Insurance Act. No free medical service but reimbursement of up to 60%. Medical insurance cards available to all enrolled on a Finnish population register.

INCOME TAX graded. *Widow supporting a child is allowed a deduction from taxable income.* Pension taxed with earnings.

CHILDREN. Special Child Allowance to children of one-parent families paid on means test, checked annually, up to age 16 or 20 for students. Family allowances for large families of limited means. Social Insurance Institution, Helsinki.

HOUSING. *There are housing subsidies which can help a widow.* Costs very different in town and country. National Board of Housing, Malminkatu 34, 00100 Helsinki 10.

EMPLOYMENT. There is unemployment in Finland at present, including in the professions. Unskilled work in shops and factories. Communes employ trained and un-trained home helpers on either full or part-time basis. *Training allowances for widows,* no earnings rule. Equal pay with men in principle. Ministry of Labour, Annankatu 25, 00100 Helsinki 10.

EDUCATION is free except for personal choice. Ministry of Education, Rauhankatu 4, 00170 Helsinki 17. Govt grants for colleges and universities, private funds and scholarships for private education.

WOMEN'S ORGANIZATIONS ETC.

Central Union of Women's Organizations, Rauhankatu 7A, 00170 Helsinki 17.
The Finnish Association of Professional and Business Women, Vuorikatu 4, 00530 Helsinki.
Union of Social Democratic Women, Paasivuorenkatu 5, 00530 Helsinki.
Zonta and Soroptomists.
British Council, Etela Esplanaadi 22, Helsinki.
Organization of the survivors of fallen soldiers.
General information from Social Welfare Boards of each locality.

BRITISH FAMILY EMERGENCY

Help from Social Welfare Boards, also British Embassy (Oudenmaankatu 16–20 Helsinki) or British consular offices at seven other towns. Reciprocal agreement with Britain on social security (DHSS leaflet SA 19).

FRANCE

(Exchange rate at May 1973:
£1 = 11·24 francs)

No statutory PENSION, various schemes for pensions exist for different occupations. Basic system (excluding agricultural workers) covers retirement and survivor's benefits, calculated on average earnings over last 10 years of work. For maximum benefit 34 years of contributions are required, from 1975 this is increased to 37½ years. War widows and industrial widows receive pension dating from death of husband; basic widow's pension paid at 65 (or 60 if invalid) as alternative to social security pension of her own. AGIRC and UNIRS schemes paid to widows aged 50 or widowed mother with at least two dependent children. Ministère de la Sécurité sociale, 8 avenue de Ségur, Paris 7e. Ministère des anciens combattants (pour les veuves de guerre), 37 rue de Bellechasse, Paris 7e.

MEDICAL benefits are provided under French scheme (Caisse Primaire de Securité Sociale). Compulsory contributions cover partial cost of doctors' fees, medicines and dentistry, and whole cost of major surgery, for insured person and dependants.

INCOME TAX. *Widowed mothers allowed tax concessions.* Pensions taxed with earnings except for war and industrial widows' pensions.

CHILDREN. Allowance of 68F monthly if father was insured, payable to age 16 (20 if student). AGIRCS and UNIRCS schemes only cover orphans who have lost both parents.

HOUSING is expensive, scarce in some areas. Mainly apartment flats to rent, but mortgages available.

EMPLOYMENT opportunities in towns for widow with typing and book-keeping skills. Without any qualification only domestic work is readily available. Minimum monthly salary 788F for a 40 hour week. Offices of Agence Nationale de l'Emploi in all areas.

SCHOOLS and lycées are free. Ministère de l'education Nationale, 110 rue de Grenelle, Paris 7e. Scholarships are awarded for further education.

WOMEN'S ORGANIZATIONS ETC.
CILAF (Comité International de Liaison des Associations Féminines), 14 Avenue Georges Mandel, Paris 16e.
UFCS (Union Féminine Civique et Sociale), 6 rue Beranger, Paris 2e.
Centre Féminin d'études et d'information, 43 rue du Faubourg St Honoré, Paris 8e.
Conseil National des Femmes, 5 rue Les Cases, Paris 7e.
Comité d'information Féminin, Association des Femmes Diplomées, l'Union Professionnelle Féminine.
Association Nationale des Veuves Civiles, 28 place St Georges, Paris 9e.
Association des Veuves de Guerre, 5 rue Ch. Colomb, Paris 8e.
Groupement spirituel des Veuves, 49 rue de la Glacière, Paris 6e.
Sindicat d'Initiatif.

Free or refunded medical treatment. Two hospitals with British staff where fees can be paid in sterling in Britain: Hertford British Hospital, 48 rue de Villiers, 92, Levallois-Perret (Paris suburb), British-American Hospital, 31–33 Blvd Maurice-Maeterlinck, Nice. Emergency help from British Embassy, 35 rue du Faubourg St Honoré, Paris 8e, British Consular offices at 14 other towns and ports.

WEST GERMANY

(Exchange rate at May 1973:
£1 = 7·00 Deutschmarks)

Widow's PENSION under social security scheme if husband had contributed for at least five years. Amount depends on age of husband at time of death, age of widow, and husband's pension base entitlement. e.g. widow under 45 whose husband was under 55 receives 0·6% for each year insured; widow over 45 receives 0·9% for each year insured (or more if her husband was older). Widowed mother under 45 is treated at over-45 rate. Civil Servants have special superannuation scheme. Automatic annual adjustment.

MEDICAL. Health Service charges are wholly or partially covered by compulsory insurance scheme, administered by nearly 2,000 independent health funds through industry. It is virtually a free health service for insured and their dependants. Federal Ministry for Health, Family and Youth Questions.

INCOME TAX. Pension taxed with earnings.

CHILDREN. Orphans' allowance for each dependent child to age 18, or 27 if student, calculated as 1/6th of pension payable to widow over 45. *Allowance continues if widow remarries*. Special Children's Allowances may be paid as alternative to Family Allowances to recipients of social benefits. Federal Ministry for Labour and Social Affairs, 5300 Bonn.

HOUSING is scarce. Govt loans and interest free Additional *Family Loans are available* for persons with two or more children building family homes or buying flats. *Rent allowances are automatic under certain income ceilings*: e.g. annual family income of 9,000 DM, increased by 1,800 DM for each further member of household.

EMPLOYMENT. Much emphasis on vocational training and re-training; under the Federal Institute for Labour *grants are readily available (with maintenance allowances and family supplements)*. Homeworkers are numerous. Employment exchanges give advice. Special provisions protect women at work. Women with their own households entitled to one free day a month. Equal pay in principle.

EDUCATION is free. Nine years full-time schooling and three years compulsory part-time vocational education. Secondary school leaving exam entitles holder to go on to university or college.

Deutscher Frauenrat, 53 Bonn, Bad Godesberg 1, Augustrasse 42, is headquarters of an association of many women's organizations, publishes *Informationen für die Frau*.

Workers' Welfare Organization, voluntary organization of help in kind.
Social Welfare group of Evangelical Church in Germany.
German Caritas Association (Roman Catholic).
Information and Advice Bureaux of the Federal Insurance Institute in most towns.
Local Sick Fund Offices give information and guidance on Health Insurance.

BRITISH FAMILY EMERGENCY
Reciprocal agreements on social security (DHSS leaflet SA 13) covers death benefit and widows' benefit but tourists are not eligible for medical benefits. Reimbursement of medical charges under terms of EEC arrangements. British Embassy, Friedrich-Ebert Allee 77, Bonn. British Consulate-General at Hamburg, Hanover, Düsseldorf, Frankfurt, Munich and Stuttgart.

HONG KONG

(Exchange rate at May 1973:
£1 = 13·12 HK dollars)

Widows' PENSION only for Civil Servants' widows aged 50 or more. No contribution qualifications, amount is calculated as percentage of salary earned. Individual industries run pension schemes, no statutory cover. Pension Section, Treasury, Hong Kong Government. Social Welfare Department, Lee Gardens 4th Floor, Hysan Avenue, Hong Kong.

Minimum rate for INCOME TAX liability HK dollar 7,000. Pension taxed with earnings.

CHILDREN. Widow and Orphan scheme (for Civil Servants only) pays allowance for unmarried dependent children to age 18 for boys, 21 for girls. No fixed rate of allowance. Public assistance on means test to other widowed mothers in need, paid up to age 15 provided child is not self-supporting.

HOUSING rents range from HK dollar 58 to 303 monthly. Population of 10,000 to the square mile. Housing Division, Urban Services Department.

EMPLOYMENT. Professional skills would need to be up-to-date for widow to practise. Factory work and semi-skilled jobs more readily available. Standard wage for women HK dollar 300–400 monthly. No earnings rule for widows. Employment Services Labour Department, Hong Kong. HK Chinese Manufacturers' Association.

EDUCATION. Primary schooling is free. Government scholarships, bursaries and donor scholarships support further education. Approximately 60% of pupils financed wholly or mostly by government.

WOMEN'S ORGANIZATIONS ETC.
The Hong Kong Kaifong Women's Association.
Hong Kong Council of Women, Room 104 Hing Fat House, 8 Duddell Street.
YWCA. Catholic Women's League.
Women's Clubs in the Community Centres.

171

General information from Neighbourhood Advisory Council.

Emergency advice from Government House, discretionary help from Social Welfare offices.

INDIA

(Exchange rate at May 1973:
£1 = 5 Rupees)

No state pension for widows. Schemes for workers earning less than 1,000 rupees a month organized by individual firms and for miners, railway and public employees. Lump sum paid as Survivor's Grant equal to total contributions paid in (including employer's share) plus 5.25% interest. Industrial injury cover provides for small widow's and orphan's pension. Better paid workers are excluded and must make private arrangements.

State programme of help-in-kind for destitute women, of two categories, promoted through existing national voluntary organizations who contribute to the cost, and organized by the Central Social Welfare Board of the Department of Education and Social Welfare. (1) To equip widowed mother with the ability to earn a living and raise family independent of the state, there are limited places in purpose-built institutions for women aged between 18 and 45 with young children. Training and vocational guidance is offered, together with food and accommodation for themselves and any children under 7 years, who receive care, medical attention and pre-school education. (2) For women aged over 45 similar institutions provide food, shelter and clothing together with recreation and simple occupation facilities.

Administration of each state under separate government. British High Commission at Chanakyapuri, New Delhi 21, Deputy High Commissioners at Bombay, Calcutta and Madras.

National Council of Women of India (and affiliated associations), Flat No 7, 54 Chawringhee Road, Calcutta 16, West Bengal.

ISRAEL

(Exchange rate at May 1973:
£1 = Israeli £10.4)

Statutory widow's PENSION on contribution qualification of two years' payments in last five years, or continuous payments for one year preceding death of insured. Full pension for widow over 50 without dependants: I£ 154.80 per month (15% of national average wage). Widowed mothers receive same, with increments for each additional child. Widow under 50 without children receives lower pension. *Widow under 40 receives lump-sum payment equivalent to two years pension. If she remarries she receives lump-sum gratuity* of 36 months' pension: if remarriage ends within 2 years she can reclaim widow's pension. National Insurance Institute, 13 Weizmann Avenue, Jerusalem.

MEDICAL Fund covers partial cost of health care and hospitalisation. If not insured in Fund those with supplementary benefit (approximately £5·8 per month if income is less than a stipulated amount) are provided with partial medical care by the state at a cost of 4% of their pension.

INCOME TAX. Widow's pension taxed with earnings.

CHILDREN. Widowed mother receives increments for her children up to age 18, up to 20 if student and up to 21 if in army. National Insurance Institute and Ministry of Social Welfare.

There is no state HOUSING scheme which would help widows. Relatives support each other, communal housing is widespread.

EMPLOYMENT readily available, full employment situation. All professions welcomed, semi-skilled and unskilled work (factories, shops and home services) and in agriculture and horticulture. Low income widows who have not previously worked may be offered vocational training by National Insurance Institute, *subsistence allowance paid during training*. Equal pay with men in theory. Ministry of Labour, Dept of Vocational Training; Rehabilitation Section, National Insurance Institute.

EDUCATION free from 5 to 15. Nat. Insurance Institute awards grant for orphans who continue with secondary education up to a certain sum of widow's earnings. Provision also for working youth age 15–18 to be released from work to complete studies. Hebrew is official language, Arabic used extensively on publications, currency and stamps. Grants for university from Ministry of Education, Shivtei Israel Street, Jerusalem.

WOMEN'S ORGANIZATIONS ETC.

Council of Women's Organizations in Israel, c/o Beth Elisheva, Moetzet Hapoaloth, 4 Elazar Hamodai Street, Jerusalem.

BRITISH FAMILY EMERGENCY

Agreement on social security between Israel and Britain covers widows' benefit and all benefits provided by British Industrial Injuries Acts (DHSS leaflet SA 14). Discretionary financial help in emergency from National Insurance Institute. British Embassy, 192 Hayarkon Street, Tel Aviv.

ITALY

(Exchange rate at May 1973:
£1 = 1,502 lire)

Widow's PENSION is paid on contribution qualification (at least 5 years of payments must have been made) under INPS scheme which covers majority of working population. Numerous separate insurance schemes also exist through industry, no uniform social security system as yet. Benefit approximately 60% of pension husband would have been entitled to. INPS (Istituto Nazionale della Providenza Soziale) Via Ciro il Grande 21, E.U.R., Roma. Automatic adjustment to cost of living.

MEDICAL costs are partially met under numerous existing schemes. Govt plans to establish National Health Service to cover whole population. INPS social security and health scheme provides a voluntary fund for housewives.

INCOME TAX PAYE system. Pension taxed with earnings.

CHILDREN's (Orphans') Allowance is 20% of father's pension entitlement for each child. If more than 2 children this 40% is shared between them. Paid up to age 18, or 26 if student.

HOUSING is largely in the form of rented apartment rooms. 3-bed-roomed flat on outskirts of Rome or other large city, medium class area, 60,000–70,000L a month.

All types of EMPLOYMENT are difficult to obtain. Dressmakers, secretaries, domestic workers for hotels in demand. Ministero del Lavoro e della Providenza Soziale, offices in all large towns.

EDUCATION free in state schools (not inclusive of books and equipment). Relatively few students obtain grants from government. Scholarships and industrial sponsored grants. Ministero della Pubblica Istruzione, Viale Trastevere, Roma.

Consiglio Nazionale delle Donne Italiane, 55 via E.Q. Visconti, Roma.
Sezione Feminile Associazione Cattolica, Via della Conciliazione, 1, Roma.
Movimento Spirituale Vedove, Via A. Monteverde 6, Roma.

BRITISH FAMILY EMERGENCY

Help from British consulate. For short-term jobs FAO in Rome employs secretarial help during conferences; private teaching of English in Italian families, English speaking shops.

JAPAN

(Exchange rate at May 1973:
£1 = 675 yen)

PENSION for widowed mothers under contributory and non-contributory schemes. Approximate pension (1973) £5 a week. Social Insurance Agency, 1–2–2 Kasumigaseki, Chiyoda-ku, Tokyo.

MEDICAL insurance contributions give free health treatment for the insured and partially free treatment for dependants.

INCOME TAX. Annual income under 180,000 yen is tax-exempted. *Widow is allowed an additional 6,000 yen.* Pension taxed with earnings.

CHILDREN'S (Orphans') allowance of approximately £1 a week per child paid to age 18. *Allowance continues if widow remarries.* National Widows' Association runs 932 Mothers' Welfare Counselling Centres, also 'Mothers' Rest Homes'.

HOUSING. Accommodation can be rented for between £1 and £5 weekly. *Low-rent public housing projects give priority to widows with children.* Japan Housing Corporation, 1–14–6 Kudankita, Chiyoda-Ku, Tokyo.

EMPLOYMENT. Professional, clerical, housekeeping, factory and shop work readily available. Widows have priority rights for running tobacco kiosks. National Widows' Association help with loans and job opportunities. Standard wage approximately £15 weekly. No Employment Bureaux, jobs through Public Employment Security Office.

EDUCATION is free, co-educational. Aid for further education from Japan Scholarship Society. English is compulsory subject in most schools. *Public officials (governors, mayors etc) stand guarantee for children of widows.* Ministry of Education, 3–2–2 Kasumigaseki, Chiyoda-ku, Tokyo.

National Widows' Association of Japan, Zenkoku Mibojin Dantai Kyogikai, 3–3–4 Kasumigaseki, Chiyoda-ku, Tokyo.
Japan Federation of Women's Organizations, 4–11–9 Sendagaya, Shibuya-ku, Tokyo.
Civilian Widows' Association, Higashi-Kuyaskushoo, Honmachi-i-Chone, Higashikui, Osaka.
YWCA, 1–8 Sorugadai, Chiyoda-ku, Tokyo.
Housewives' Federation.
Professor Kiyoshi Ikegawa, Nakatsu-Riverside House A–1330, 3 Nakatsu-Hamadori 1 chome, Oyodo-ku, Osaka (Friend of Cruse).

BRITISH FAMILY EMERGENCY

Help from Welfare Ministry, Metropolitan and other local government offices. English-speaking doctors and dentists may be contacted on application to hotels. No reciprocal arrangement with Britain on social security. British Embassy, Ichiban-cho, Kojimachi, Chiyoda-ku, Tokyo. British Consulates at Osaka, Yokohama, Nagoya and Kita Kyushu.

MALTA

(Exchange rate at May 1973:
£1 = Maltese £0·9)

Widows' PENSION paid if husband was insured under 1956 National Insurance Act and had paid required contributions. Minimum amount £M1·50 weekly, maximum £M3·00 (1973). Dept of Social Services, 310 Kingsway, Valletta, Malta.

MEDICAL. Only those who are receiving industrial injury benefit or disablement benefit are entitled to free medical and hospital treatment. Subsidised charges for others under National Insurance scheme.

INCOME TAX. Rate of tax 10c in the £ for first £200 of taxable income, rising to 38c in the £. Pension taxed with earnings with exception of war and disability pensions.

CHILDREN'S Allowance approximately £M0·35 weekly, paid to age 16. Dept of Social Services, 310 Kingsway, Valletta.

HOUSING. Government flats sometimes available, normally 5-roomed, leased at approximately £M80·00 per annum. The Housing Secretary, Housing Dept, Sa Maison Road, Pieta, Malta.

EMPLOYMENT. Professional qualifications helpful. British medical and nursing qualifications recognised. No earnings rule for widows.

EDUCATION free, children are taught in Maltese and English. Limited aid from government for certain further education courses. Education Dept, 32/33 Marsamxetto Road, Valletta.

National Council of Women of Malta, 38/5 Old Mint Street, Valletta.
Women's Corona Society.
Women's Catholic Action, Catholic Institute, Floriana.
Social Assistance Secretariat, Catholic Institute, Floriana.
International Council of Women.

Contact should be made with British High Commission, 7 St Anne Street, Floriana. Reciprocal social security arrangements with Britain (DHSS leaflet SA 11).

NÈTHERLANDS

(Exchange rate at May 1973:
£1 = Dfl. 7·25)

Statutory PENSION on contribution qualification to widows from 40 years, widowed mothers and incapacitated widows. Amount, as Old Age Pension, Dfl. 447 monthly, with *Holiday Allowance paid annually* in May. Automatic adjustment to cost of living increases. Social Security Information Centre, Rhijnspoorplein 1, Amsterdam. Gemeenschappelijk Administratiekantoor, Bos en Lommerplantseen, Amsterdam.

State MEDICAL insurance entitles insured to free medical treatment, up to 70 days free hospitalisation, full dental care and partial cost of dentures. Administered by Algemeen Nederlands Onderling Ziekenfonds, Kromme Nieuwegracht 56, Utrecht.

INCOME TAX minimum limit fixed on yearly basis. Widow pays tax on pension.

CHILDREN. Orphan's allowance only if both parents are dead (Dfl. 186 monthly to age 16 or 27 if student). Local Councils for the Protection of Children.

HOUSING can be rented for £12 upwards a week. Mortgages possible. Netherlands is most densely populated country in world. Local Housing Bureaux in municipalities.

EMPLOYMENT. Any qualification an asset. Domestic and shop work available according to labour market. Minimum wage of Dfl. 198·60 weekly for employees between 23 and 65 years. No earnings rule for widows. Fewer women go out to work than in any other EEC country. Local Government Labour Offices advise on job possibilities.

EDUCATION. Small charge made for nursery education (to age 6). No charge from 6 to 15 years, after that fees are assessed according to means, payable up to annual limit. Government grants system for further education. Ministry of

Education & Science, Nieuwe Uitleg 1, The Hague.

Nederlandse Vereniging voor Vrouwenbelangen, Balbaostraat 3, Amsterdam.
  Vereniging 'Onderlinge Vrouwenbescherming', Groene Wetering 42, Rotter-
  dam 16.
Stichting Nederlandse Federatie voor Vrouwelijke Vrijwillige Hulpverlening,
  Pieter Bothastraat 27, Den Haag.
Union of Women Voluntary Helpers.
Union of Professional Women, of Country Women, of Housewives (equivalent to
  Women's Institute).
Netherlands Widows and Widowers League (Weduwen an Weduwnaars Bond,
  Rotterdam Post Box 8065.

BRITISH FAMILY EMERGENCY

Advice and financial help where needed from Municipal Social Service offices.
Special social security arrangements with Britain (DHSS leaflet SA 7).

NEW ZEALAND

(Exchange rate at May 1973:
£1 = 2 NZ dollars)

Widows' PENSION paid on means test to widowed mothers and over 50's. No
contribution requirements but certain residential requirements required. Widow
without child receives approximately NZ dollars 21·00, widow with one child NZ
dollars 32·00: for each additional child NZ dollars 1·25 weekly. Dept of Social
Welfare, Wellington, NZ.
  MEDICAL. Treatment in hospital and prescriptions are free under NZ Health
Service. Doctors' and specialists' fees partially refunded, dental treatment free
only for children. Dept of Health, Wellington.
  INCOME TAX minimum rate NZ dollars 572, $780 for widowed mother.
Income rule reduces pension of widowed mother if income exceeds NZ dollars 624
per annum: for a widow without children income limit is $520. Pension is not taxed
with earnings.
  CHILDREN. Orphans' allowance only if both parents are dead. Family allowance of NZ dollars 3·00 weekly for each child paid to age 16. Dept of Social Welfare, Wellington.
  HOUSING. Rents approx £10 weekly. *Special 3% house purchase loan scheme*
for those with limited resources. *State Advances.* Corporation of NZ, PO Box
5009, Wellington.
  EMPLOYMENT. Doctors, teachers, nurses, secretaries etc in demand. Factory
work, shop work, cleaning jobs depending on labour market. Local agencies listed
in Yellow Pages. Dept of Labour, PO Box 6310, Teare, Wellington.
  EDUCATION free, private schools also. Dept of Education for school grants,
University Grants Committee for further education. Dept of Education Private
Bag 2, Wellington.

WOMEN'S ORGANIZATIONS ETC.

National Council of Women of NZ, PO Box 9167, Wellington.
YWCA, 33 Tory Street, Wellington 1.
Dominion Federation of Townswomen's Guilds.
Association of Anglican Women, PO Box 957, Wellington.
Association of Presbyterian Women.
Catholic Women's League.
Birthright (society to support one-parent families), PO Box 347, Wellington. Also Room 314, Victoria Arcade, Shortland Street, Auckland and 43 Stanbury Avenue, Christchurch.
Ombudsman, Parliamentary Commissioner for Investigations, Mayfair Chambers, 48 The Terrace, Wellington 1.

BRITISH FAMILY EMERGENCY

Medical treatment available to British visitors on same terms as residents. UK pension entitlements will be paid under reciprocal arrangements (DHSS leaflet SA 8). Emergency help from Social Security offices (Aotea Quay, Wellington, and elsewhere). British High Commission, Customhouse Quay, Wellington C1.

NORWAY

(Exchange rate at May 1973: £1 = 14·55 kroner)

PENSION for widowed mothers and over 40's. Separate schemes for seamen, fishermen, foresters and civil servants. Minimum period of 3 years insurance is required, full basic pension requires 40 years of contributions. Maximum amount approx. N.Kr 8,000 annually (also paid to widowers). Pensions adjusted to cost of living. Rikstrygdeverket, Drammensveiew 60, Oslo 2.

MEDICAL benefits under Health Insurance Scheme cover treatment and dentistry, certain drugs, in-patient care in hospital, home nursing costs, hearing aids, and transport to doctor or hospital. Ministry of Social Affairs (Socialdepartementet) Oslo.

INCOME TAX minimum N.Kr 7,000 annually. Widows' Pension not taxed with earnings but subject to earnings rule.

CHILDREN under 18 receive Orphans' Benefit: 40% of father's basic pension entitlement for first child, 25% for each other child. Ministry of Social Affairs, Ministry of Family and Consumer Affairs.

HOUSING. National Insurance scheme makes provision for grants and loans to cover expenses connected with travelling or moving house for purpose of obtaining paid employment.

EMPLOYMENT. *National Insurance covers re-training courses. Assistance benefit may be paid to widow who must leave her children in care while training or working; also transitional benefit if she is temporarily unable to earn a living on account of her children.* Widows' Pension subject to earnings rule.

EDUCATION is free between ages 7 and 16. Secondary education provided by

state, local authorities and privately. Grants from government for university, industrial and technical institute courses. Dept of Church and Education, Oslo.

National Council of Women of Norway, Norske Kvinners Nasjonalrad, Fr. Nan-
    sensplass 6, Oslo 1.
YWCA.

Medical benefits under reciprocal scheme (DHSS leaflet SA 16) cover free hospital
treatment for visitors and partial reimbursement of doctor's and out-patient dept.
charges. All benefits provided by British National Insurance, Industrial Injuries
Acts and Family Allowances are covered by the agreement. British Embassy, 8
Thomas Heftyes Gate, Oslo 2. British Consular offices at 10 other towns.

SOUTH AFRICA

(Exchange rate at May 1973:
£1 = 1·8 Rands)

No general statutory PENSION. Available for widowed mother on means test:
monthly allowance of 32 rands for white widow, R.13·75 for coloured widow,
R.2·55 for African widow. Old age pension payable at 60 (through industrial
schemes) R.41 for whites, R.20 for coloureds. Dept of Social Welfare and Pensions, Huguenot Bldg, Queen Victoria Street, Cape Town (and branches in all
towns in the Republic).
　　MEDICAL. No health service or social security. Individual firms arrange medical insurance and health charges are met according to personal means. Africans
charged little or nothing for medicines.
　　INCOME TAX at 9% for widow, who is *taxed as a married woman*. Overseas
pension is not taxed, S. African pensions taxed with earnings.
　　A Maintenance Grant is paid for widows' CHILDREN if income is inadequate.
Approximately R.11 per month for each of first 3 children, with lower rate for subsequent children, plus R.6 monthly for each school-going child. Allowance payable until schooling ends. Child Welfare Commissioner, Dept of Social Welfare
and Pensions, also Society for the Protection of Child Life, Garmor House, Plein
Street, Cape Town.
　　HOUSING. Pre-war accommodation rent-controlled. Usually long waiting list
for rented flats, minimum R.80 a month. Mortgage possible but widow must sign a
Bond accepting financial responsibility of a man and forfeiting her 'protective
rights' as a woman. i.e. if payments are in default she can be imprisoned. The Cape
Town Municipality has economic accommodation, Divisional Council has home-
ownership schemes. The Citizens' Housing League Utility Co, is a non-profit-
making company with reasonably priced houses.
　　EMPLOYMENT. Qualifications helpful. Bilingualism usually required. Unskilled work in distributive trade. No standard wage. Examples: qualified shop
assistants average R.115 monthly, experienced typist R.180, qualified hairdresser
R.135 plus commission of 20–40%.

EDUCATION is free generally, varies for coloureds and Africans. Grants through the State, also scholarships and bursaries. Provincial Education Dept, Provincial Administration Bldg, Wale Street, Cape Town (also in Orange Free State, Transvaal and Natal).

National Council of Women of S. Africa, 4th Floor, CTC Bldg, Plein Street, Cape Town.
YWCA, Andrew Murray House Gardens, Cape Town.
The Widows' Information Service, 532 CTC Bldg, Plein Street, Cape Town.
'The Go it Alone' Club, 30 Cambridge Street, Farramere, Benoni, Transvaal.
Citizens' Advice Bureaux.

In bereavement or other crisis emergency help from Dept of Social Welfare, Huguenot Bldg, Queen Victoria Street, Cape Town. Also from Settlers' Club, the Victoria League, and the British Consulate. No reciprocal agreement with UK on social security.

SPAIN

(Exchange rate at May 1973:
£1 = 147·70 pesetas)

PENSION payable to widow nationals over 40 and widowed mothers on contribution qualification. Amount is percentage of husband's basic wages. Minimum pay level fixed by law for each of 12 occupational groups (e.g. lowest salary-paid group: Ptas. 4,680 per month). Special systems for civil servants, agricultural workers and seamen. Ministry: Instituto Nacional de Previsión, Alcala 56, Madrid.

MEDICAL insurance scheme under social security system provides partial cover for prescriptions and medical care for insured and his dependants.

INCOME TAX minimum liability of Ptas. 75·000 per annum, standard rate 10%. *Pension not taxed with earnings.*

CHILDREN receive Orphans' allowance, approximately 20% of father's basic wage, with minimum of Ptas. 250 per month, payable to age 18. Instituto Nacional de Previsión.

HOUSING. Rents approximately Ptas. 800 weekly in towns. Mortgages can be taken out by women. Ministerio de la Vivienda, Madrid.

EMPLOYMENT. Qualifications helpful. Unskilled work according to labour market. No basic rights for women in law, education and pay. No earnings rule for widows. Christian Communities for Widows and Widows' Associations run training schemes, employment bureaux and nursery schools. Job vacancies found through Ministerio de Trabajo, Madrid (and branch offices) or Organizacion Sindical Espanola.

EDUCATION free. Grants for further education from Delegaciones and

Provincial departments of Ministerio de Educacion y Ciencia, Madrid.

WOMEN'S ORGANIZATIONS ETC.

Delegacion Nacional de la Seccion Femenina, Almagro 34, Madrid (for the training and promotion of women generally).

Comunidad Cristiana de Viudas, Hurtago de Amezaga 8, Bilbao 8 and Maldonado 1, Madrid.

Asociaciones de Viudas en Espana (Widows' Associations): Ana Maria Ruiz-Rivas, Viuda de Carre President, Jose Ortega y Gasset 23, Madrid 6, and many branches.

General information: Organizacion Sindical, Paseo del Prado 18, Madrid.

BRITISH FAMILY EMERGENCY

No reciprocal agreement with UK on social security. British-American hospital at Calle Limite, Madrid, open day and night. British Embassy, Calle Fernando el Santo 16, Madrid. British Consular offices at 19 other Spanish towns.

SWEDEN

(Exchange rate at May 1973:
£1 = 11·10 Swedish Kronor)

Full Widows' PENSION for over 50's, approximately S.Kr 540 monthly. Marriage must have lasted 5 years and husband's contributions qualify. *Smaller graduated rates paid from age 36 and to widowed mothers of any age. Pension may be restored if remarriage occurs and is ended within 5 years.* Pensions adjusted to cost of living. Riksförsäkringsverket, Fack, Stockholm 7.

MEDICAL cover under Swedish sickness insurance scheme provides free inpatient hospital treatment, 3/4 refund of doctors' fees, certain drugs (not dentistry). Free health care for children to age 16. Riksförsäkringsanstalten, Adolf Fredriks Kyrkogata 8, Stockholm 3.

INCOME TAX. Pensions taxed with earnings but *Family Allowances (for children to age 16) not liable for tax.*

CHILDREN receive Orphan's benefit of approximately S.Kr 180 monthly to age 16 (25 if student). If father died from industrial injury child has annuity of 1/6th of his earnings to age 19.

HOUSING. *State rent allowance for widows.* Majority of families own two homes. Housing depts in each of the 24 local government districts.

EMPLOYMENT prospects for women made easier by *widespread provision of day-nurseries, whole-day care from 6 months to 6 years as required*, nursery schooling for 4–7 year-olds, all for small charge. *Holidays in camps* for older children can be arranged free or at reduced cost for *widows' children.* Secretarial and other skills in demand. Training and refresher courses. Unskilled work in agriculture, shops and factories, or helping in youth camps.

EDUCATION is free from age 7 to 16 in Grundskolan, further education in Gymnasia. Free school meals, books and supplies. State grants for university. Dept of Education, Stockholm.

Information on the Welfare State and local organizations from: The Swedish Institute, Box 7072, S–103 82 Stockholm 7.
National Council of Women of Sweden, Svenska Kvinnors Nationalforbund, Valhallavagen 131, 115 31 Stockholm.
YWCA.

BRITISH FAMILY EMERGENCY

Benefits under reciprocal agreement with UK (DHSS leaflet SA 9) include medical treatment under same terms as Swedish nationals. Family Allowances payable to British family in Sweden provided child is living there and one parent is registered there. British Embassy in Stockholm, Consular offices at Gävle, Göteborg, Helsingborg, Luteå, Malmö, Norrköping and Sundsvall.

SWITZERLAND

*(Exchange rate at May 1973:
£1 = Swiss Francs 7·91)*

Statutory PENSION to widowed mothers and widows aged 40 and over who have been married at least 5 years, on husband's contribution qualification. *Swiss Special Pensions for those ineligible.* Maximum Widows' Pension is 80% of retirement pension for single person, Swiss Fr. 4,224 per annum. *Widow ineligible may be paid lump sum.* Automatic adjustment to cost of living. Caisse Suisse de Compensation, rue des Pâquis 52, 1200 Geneva. Caisse de l'Assurance Vieillesse et Survivants.

MEDICAL. Membership of one of the many Swiss sickness insurance funds carries entitlement to most medical care and prescriptions (not dentistry). Office Federal des Assurances Sociales, Effingerstrasse 33, Berne.

INCOME TAX. Federal tax is levied as well as Cantonal and Communal tax. Pension taxed with earnings.

CHILDREN. Orphans' allowance if father's contributions qualify, paid to age 18 or 25. Maximum amount Sw.Fr. 2,112 per annum. Caisse Suisse de Compensation.

HOUSING. Accommodation very variable in cost, rather expensive. Mainly flats to buy or rent.

EMPLOYMENT. Labour market is protected for residents by quota limit for foreign workers. No earnings rule for widows. *Re-training schemes.* Applications for work by British must be made *before* an 'Assurance of a Residence' permit can be issued. Those who have entered Switzerland as temporary visitors will be refused work permit and application reconsidered only after they have left the country.

EDUCATION free from age 7 to 14 or 15, controlled by individual Cantons and Communes. The Swiss Foundation for Young People gives help for further education.

WOMEN'S ORGANIZATIONS ETC.
British-Swiss Society in Berne and Zürich.
National Council of Women of Switzerland (Alliance de Sociétés Féminines Suisses,) Mainaustrasse 12, CH–8008, Zürich.
YWCA in many localities. Local church organizations.

BRITISH FAMILY EMERGENCY
Under reciprocal agreement (DHSS leaflet SA 6) widow's benefit under UK scheme is payable; if husband was insured under both British and Swiss schemes widow is herself working in a state organization she cannot receive pension from ate at Berne, Zürich, Geneva, Basel, Montreux or Lugano.

TURKEY

(Exchange rate at May 1973:
£1 = Turkish lira 34)

No statutory PENSION, only for widows of state institution employees. If a widow is herself working in a state organization she cannot receive pension from husband. Monthly payment calculated on husband's earnings. Widowed mother is paid more. No age restrictions. State authority: Sosyal Sigortalar Kurumu Genel Müdürlüğü, Ankara. Emekli Sandigi Genel Müdürlüğü, Ankara. Bağ-Kur Genel Müdürlüğü, Ankara.

MEDICAL insurance through Turkish sickness insurance scheme provides for free medical care for certain prescribed periods for insured and dependants.

INCOME TAX according to subsistence level, specified every year. Pension is taxed with earnings if not in state employ.

Allowance for widow's CHILDREN paid to her as part of her pension if husband was state employee. Continues for girls until marriage, for boys until 18 or university graduation (ends if widow remarries). State Children's Welfare Organization: Sağlik ve Sosyal Yardim Bakanliği, Sosyal Hizmetler Genel Müdürlüğü, Goouk Refahi Subesí, Sihhiye, Ankara.

State HOUSING authority: Imar ve Iskân Bakanliği, Mesken Genel Müdürlüğü, Ankara.

EMPLOYMENT. Secretarial, nursing and catering qualifications helpful. Unskilled jobs in local industries (cotton, woollen and silk textiles, cosmetics, foodstuffs) and in agriculture. Employment authority: Calisma Bakanliği, Is ve Isci Bulma Kürumu, Sihhiye, Ankara.

EDUCATION is predominantly free and secular. State scholarships, state and private charity grants for further education to universities and Faculty of Agriculture. Education authority: Milli Egitom, Bakanliği, Bakanliklar, Ankara.

WOMEN'S ORGANIZATIONS ETC.
Türk Kadurlar Konseyl, Posta Kutusu 44, Yenisehir, Ankara.
Türk Kadinlar Borligi
Universiteli Kadinlar Borligi
Türk Ev Kadinlar Dunigi

Turkish Mothers' Association

BRITISH FAMILY EMERGENCY
British Embassy at Ankara, British Consular offices at Istanbul, Izmir and Iskenderun. Reciprocal Social Security agreement with Britain (DHSS leaflet SA 22) covers widows' benefits and death grant. Local voluntary associations in Turkey usually help in a crisis.

U.S.A.

(Exchange rate at May 1973:
£1 = 2·5 dollars)

PENSION paid to widow if husband was insured under social security system (now compulsory for all residents except casual workers and some self-employed). Widow aged 62 or more is paid 82·5% of husband's pension entitlement; widowed mothers under 62 are paid 75%; widows aged 50–62 or disabled widows are paid 50–80%. Special systems for civil service and railroad employees. *Pension may be reinstated if a subsequent remarriage ends.* US Dept of Health, Education and Welfare, Washington.

MEDICAL benefits only free to pensioners over 65. State-run Public Health Service Insurance schemes provide for partial costs of hospital and health care, which without insurance cover are extremely high.

INCOME TAX. Taxpayer identification no. issued to each social security beneficiary, p.a.y.e. *Allowances for different categories include child care expenses for working mother.* Pension taxed with earnings, and subject to earnings rule.

CHILDREN'S pension is 75% of father's basic pension entitlement to age 18, 22 if student. Unless child is disabled this ends on remarriage of mother.

HOUSING authority: Dept of Housing and Urban Development (departments in each state).

EMPLOYMENT opportunities for all ages. Professional women have headstart. Part-time or seasonal work widely available in cotton textile industry, farms, hotels, private households, restaurants, libraries, holiday camps. Programs of vocational training and refresher courses at colleges may include counselling, job placement, nursery facilities and grants through Federal govts. *Federal grants-in-aid to State public welfare agencies for daycare services to help working mothers, priority to low-income families.* 31 States have equal pay laws. Non-whites disadvantaged occupationally. All social security benefits subject to earnings rule.

EDUCATION is free to age 16. Qualifications, from high school diploma upwards, are needed for most jobs. Educational opportunity grants for full-time students in financial need from Federal government. Also annual loans to be repaid after studies are completed. Fellowships and scholarships (e.g. teaching, counselling, nursing) from US Dept of Health, Education & Welfare. Neighbourhood Youth Corps offers part-time and summer jobs/training to those under 22 who could not otherwise afford to stay on at school.

WOMEN'S ORGANIZATIONS ETC.
General Federation of Women's Clubs, 1734 N St NW, Washington DC.

National Council of Women of US Inc, 345 E 46th St, New York.
YWCA, 600 Lexington Avenue, New York.
Altrusa International Inc, 332 S Michigan Avenue, Chicago (grants for women for re-training or starting a business).
Family Service of Westchester, 131 Court St, White Plains, NY (special services for widows).
NAIM Conference (Roman Catholic), 109 Dearborn St, Chicago, Ill. (self-help for widows and widowers).
Theos Foundation (Lutheran women), 125 Veronica Drive, Pittsburgh, Pa. (for widows).

BRITISH FAMILY EMERGENCY

British Embassy, 3100 Massachusetts Avenue, NW, Washington DC. Discretionary help from state Welfare departments. No reciprocal agreement with Britain on social security.

ADDENDA

page 26   In 1974 the Chancellor of the Exchequer gave notice of a proposed Gift Tax, to be backdated to the March 1974 Budget.
page 129   'Singlehanded Ltd' is a new and courageous attempt to meet the problems of single parents, men or women, and bring them together to share homes and families. Organizer, Mrs Anne Kavanagh, 68 Lewes Road, Haywards Heath, Sussex.
page 160   1974 Widows' Pensions (Great Britain): Widow's Allowance (first 26 weeks) £14 a week. Standard Widow's Pension and Widowed Mother's Allowance £10. Widow's Basic Pension £3. Widow's Children: weekly allowance of £4.90 for each child, including Family Allowances.

INDEX

188